OFFICERS and SOLDIERS o

THE FRENCH IMPERIAL GUARD 1804-1815

Volume 3
The Cavalry

Part Two

André JOUINEAU

translated from the French by
Alan McKAY

HISTOIRE & COLLECTIONS

The CAVALRY of the IMPERIAL GUARD

After having dealt with the older regiments of the cavalry of the Guard in the preceding volume, in this book we will be looking at the units which, at the turning point of the Empire, best incarnated the universal character which Napoleon had wanted for his political edifice. Foreigners in the very heart of the unit entrusted with protecting him, what better proof of the trust he placed in the Poles, Dutch or in the Lithuanians…

The Mamelukes

General Bonaparte who was careful of his "Roman Consul" image liked to colour this image with the mysteries of the Orient. He did not hesitate to make use of the "oriental" trend which was greatly in fashion in France after the Expeditionary Force to Egypt returned. Thus, following on the Chasseurs à cheval, the Company of Mamelukes was created in the Consular Guard; it was the last evocation of the Egyptian Campaign. When the Empire started, these troops were fully incorporated into the Imperial Guard.

The Lancers

As the policy of conquest developed further and further, entire regiments of "European" origin joined the Guard. The Poles were the first. A number of Prince Poniatowski's compatriots had already joined in the revolutionary forces in the hope of restoring the old Polish monarchy with the help of the young Republic and then the Empire and free it from the weight of the Austrian and Tsarist yoke.

It was the Poles, first of all with the Chevau-Légers, who re-introduced the lance into the French cavalry after the 1809 campaign. (*)

On 1 July 1810 Louis, Napoleon's oldest brother, who was the King of Holland, abdicated. Dutch troops were immediately incorporated into the Imperial Army. The citizens of the former Batavian Republic also furnished a second regiment of Lancers, created from the Hussars of the Royal Dutch Guard. During

---

(*) The Lancers, as a subdivision of the Cavalry, were created at this time and they only disappeared with the fall of the Second Empire in 1870. Even then, the lance was not abandoned and was used by the Dragoons right up to the end of the First World War.

the Russian campaign, the Guard needed new troops. Occupying Lithuania enabled a 3rd Lancer regiment to be created but with a much shorter life.

Joachim Murat, Maréchal de France and member of the Imperial Family was made Grand-Duke of Cleves-Berg in 1806. the Grand-Duchy united two German provinces, administered from Paris which entered the Rhine Confederation after Jena. As a counterpart, the Grand-Duchy ensured that troops were levied for the Empire, with a contingent of 5 000 men.

Murat hoping to exchange a Duke's title against a King's crown set off for Spain and created a corps of lancers which followed him over the Pyrenees. There was no Spanish crown for Joachim but rather a Neapolitan one instead. The new Berg Lancers, who remained in Spain, joined the Imperial Guard and ended their adventure at Leipzig in 1813.

The Gendarmes

The Gendarmerie d'Elite Legion was created with the Consular Guard. It was entrusted with the protection of the imperial palaces and campaign headquarters: wherever Napoleon and his entourage were. Moreover, it was given responsibility for all the Provost's tasks within the Guard.

The Guard as a nursery for cadres

The officers and the NCOs with any education were not legion in the Grande Armée. In spite of the creation of the Ecole Spéciale Militaire at Saint-Cyr (near Versailles), and the Ecole de cavalerie at Saint Germain, the training of officers became increasingly problematic as the losses and the need to replace them increased in Napoleon's army. The Guard tried to deal with this problem in two ways.

– The Velites attached to the Cavalry of the Guard units enabled the NCOs and Sub-Lieutenants to be trained and then assigned rapidly to regiments of the Line. They were young people who had some education benefiting from income. When campaigning they were incorporated into the units they were assigned to and wore its uniform. The regiments who accepted the Velites were the Grenadiers à cheval, the Chasseurs à cheval and the 2nd Chevau-Léger

Regiment. In peacetime these Velites were separated from the rest of the troops and followed their own course of training. The system in fact created a "practical military school". Most of these young people became officers in the Line. Maréchal Bugeaud started his career like that.

– For the infantry, the Ecole de Fontainebleau whose instructors were officers and NCOs of the Guard and instructed Corporals and Sergeants of the Line.

The "intellectual" arm – the Artillery – already had its training infrastructure, ever since the Ancien Régime and the Revolution had not altered its system.

The old veterans who had at least ten years' service continued to serve in the Guard. At the apogee of the Empire, they already had twenty years of campaigning behind them; nearly all of them had been awarded the "cross" but without knowing how to neither read nor write, they could not rise up in the military hierarchy. The old soldiers, as and when they retired ended up in the Gendarmerie for the lucky ones, or in household jobs or at the Invalides.

The Guard was also a mixture of the nations of Europe who were allies of the Empire. At the time of Napoleon's marriage to Marie-Louise, Dutch, Poles, Belgians, Italians, Rhinelanders, Swiss, Armenians, etc., were to be found in the Imperial Guard. The Guard was present in the Spanish sierras, on the distant marches of Germany. Only the depot battalions were stationed within and around Paris while the combat battalions covered the Empire, "pushing the stones" along the roads of Europe.

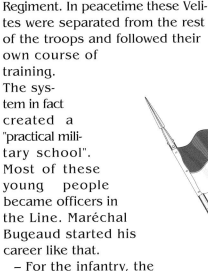

The Guard – a psychological weapon

Since it was created, the strength of the Guard increased throughout the Empire, going from 9 798 men in 1804 to 56 169 in 1812. This unit became the supreme reserve confronting the Russian threat, even if this threat appeared more, or less, pressing after the treaties (Tilsitt) or the interviews (Erfurt).

Unfortunately Alexander I never disarmed. For napoleon, his Guard remained a determining element in his 1812 invasion plans. Paradoxically, the Guard was hardly used until Moscow.

Although its feats of arms in Spain, at Austerlitz, Eylau, or Wagram rather proved its worth, the Guard was rarely committed. Its presence alone on the battlefield was enough to produce a terrible psychological effect on the enemy's morale whilst at the same time inspiring the other French troops. Unfortunately for the "team spirit" within the body of the Grande Armée – and this feature became more and more noticeable over the years – the Guard remained a privileged corps benefiting from immense advantages and this was the cause of real jealousy within the ranks of the Line regiments. The Guard was the main reserve force during the whole of the French campaign, at Montmirail, Vauchamps or Champaubert. On the other hand, at Waterloo, its hesitation, its holding back – one can even say its flight – threw the last heroes over the precipice...

The MAMELUKES

In 1801, a small group of horsemen landed at Marseilles with a large number of Egyptian refugees; they were Mamelukes who had served in the French Army during the Egyptian Campaign. They were born in Syria, most of them but there were also some from Georgia, Circassia, Crimea, Armenia, Arabia, Anatolia, Egypt, Abyssinia, Darfur. Others came from the Balkans, Hungary, Albania, Malta, Tunisia or even Algeria. Some of them had come alone, others with their families.

On 13 October, Bonaparte decided to create a "*squadron of Mamelukes which would accompany the person of the First Consul without being part of the Consular Guard*". The Mamelukes and their families were organised and billeted at Melun. French officers and NCOs were responsible for the administration and training. On 12 October 1802, the Mamelukes were incorporated into the Consular Guard following the *Chasseurs à cheval*. The creation of the Imperial Guard did not modify their status and the company was still administered by the Chasseurs à cheval Regiment. A decree dated 15 April 1806 sent all the Mamelukes' families and those who had quit the service to live in Marseilles.

The Mamelukes took part in all the Empires campaigns. Their first exploit was during the charge of the *Chasseurs à cheval* against Alexander's Horse Guards at Austerlitz. During the Polish Campaign they were engaged at Pultsuk, Golymin and Eylau.

They were then sent to Spain and became sadly famous at Madrid during the "Dos de Mayo" (2 May 1808) demonstrations. They took part in the Battle of Medina del Rio Secco. Returning from Spain to ride around along the banks of the Niemen, the squadron entered Moscow alongside the *Chasseurs à cheval*. Subsequently the Mamelukes took part in all the fighting during the retreat from Russia, the Saxon Campaign and finally the French Campaign. After the Restoration, the Mamelukes were still attached to the *Chasseurs à Cheval* of the Guard, which had become the *Corps Royal des Chasseurs à Cheval de France*. On Elba the "Napoleon Squadron" comprised some Mamelukes.

During the Hundred Days, the Mamelukes charged one final time with the Chasseurs à cheval of the Guard. At the end of July 1815, they were dismissed at Libourne and Agen.

A large number of these veterans and their families were massacred by the population in Marseilles. The rare Mamelukes who remained in France lived in total precariousness; the royal administration did not recognise their veteran's status and as a result did not hand over the least franc of the half pay to which they were entitled.

Strength

The number of Mamelukes went up and down with time. In January 1802, they were organised into a squadron of 150 men. In October there were 172. In December 1803, the numbers were reorganised into a company and dropped to 114, then to 109 in July 1804. During the Prussian Campaign, in 1806, they were a squadron again with 13 officers and 147 men. In January 1807, the strength was 10 officers and 106 men (74 in June). In 1808, during the Spanish Campaign, the company consisted of 86 men. After 1809, the company that left for Russia comprised 109 men.

Between 1809 and 1813, fifty or so Mamelukes of non-eastern origin started to be incorporated into the company. In March 1813, the Mamelukes were organised into a squadron of 250 men. The eastern and the French Mamelukes taken into the Line were the "First Mamelukes" (Old Guard), the others recruited in France or in different European countries were "Second Mamelukes" (Young Guard). Between 1813 and 1814, 205 Frenchmen and 119 Europeans were incorporated into the squadron.

At the Restoration there were only 18 real Mamelukes left. Only 41 Mamelukes of the Old Guard remained in the Royal Corps of Chasseurs. During the Hundred Days, the Mamelukes were organised into a squadron with two companies.

Dress: Wealth and Fantasy...

The decree dated 25 Germinal An X (15 April 1802) *stipulated: "the dress and the weapons of the Corps of Mamelukes would be what they wore in Egypt. They would be mounted like light troops and as a reward for the loyalty to the French Army, they would wear the green cahuk and white turban"*.

In fact, there was complete anarchy and permanent fantasy in the Mameluke's uniforms which lasted right up to 1815. One needs only to consult the reports on the state of dress. There was an infinite variety and wealth of cloth, colour and articles of haberdashery which had no equal in any other corps. In order to be a bit more clear we will try to detail below the typically "oriental" elements of this dress.

Head Dress: this was composed of the *cahuk*, a sort of green, yellow or red cap; or the *tarbush* which was a flat chechia, always red. Both these were surrounded at their base with a *shal*, a white cotton turban which differed with each head dress. There exists also a cahuk with sides and a hollow crown. It was sometimes decorated with a brass crescent. From 1806, the cahuk replaced the tarbush which was only worn with the service dress. From 1809 to 1815, the cahuk evolved: the sides were removed as was the hollow crown; it had now the shape of a red shako without a peak. The front was decorated with a star surmounting a crescent or a tricolour cockade. It had a double puff or a pompom. There was also a cahuk cover.

Dress: there was the *banish*, a robe with very ample sleeves which disappeared around 1808 to be replaced by narrower European-style sleeves; the *mantanna*, a sort of Greek tunic also had sleeves; sleeveless waistcoats, the *fermelet* and the *yalek*. These various items could be tailored out of different types and colours of cloth. The very baggy Turkish trousers, called the *sharual*, were crimson, amaranthine or white.

A sash belt worn over the rest of the uniform held the *kubur*, a worked leather sheath holding two pistols; the Mamelukes were also issued with a mixed grey coat. The boots were made of different coloured leather and had no spurs. These only appeared in 1809 with the recruitment of non-Eastern Mamelukes.

Towards 1809, the Mamelukes were issued with an imperial blue (sky blue for the trumpeters) forage cap with crimson piping and with a stripe decorated with a crescent. Towards the end of 1812, the yalek and the coat had sleeves. The clothing reports mention riding breeches with sheepskin, but this was most likely distributed to the "French" Mamelukes of the Young Guard.

"French-style" uniforms

After 1804, the Mameluke officers and the NCOs wore a so-called "society uniform": tail-coat exactly the same as that worn by the *Chasseurs à Cheval*: it was imperial blue with crimson distinctives; the turnbacks were decorated with crescents. The waistcoat was crimson and the "Hungarian-style" trousers were blue. In this uniform they wore a hat. They were also issued with a pelisse with gold braid for the officers, yellow for the NCOs, with riding breeches with sheepskin with crimson side stripes and a frock-coat. Golden aglets mixed with blue were for the NCOs.

The Trumpeters and the Musicians

The trumpeters wore a sky-blue banish. This was not however always the case. As well as their "oriental" dress, they received an identical uniform to that described above but sky blue with mixed gold and crimson braid and aglets. The "Turkish" musicians were known although not mentioned on the roll. It comprised seven musicians: 2 cymbalists, two Jingling Johnnies, 2 tambourines and a timpanist. The uniforms were not different apparently from those worn by the ordinary cavalryman.

The MAMELUKES in 1804

When the Imperial Guard was created, the Mameluke Company comprised:

Headquarters
(French)
— 1 Captain Commanding
— 1 Health Officer
— 1 Adjutant Sub-Lieutenant
— 1 *Maréchal des logis chef*
— 1 Fourrier
— 1 Veterinary Officer
— 1 Master-Saddler
— 1 Master-Tailor
— 1 Master-Cobbler
The Company
— 2 Captains
— 2 First-Lieutenants
— 2 Second-lieutenants
— 2 Trumpeters
— 8 *Maréchaux des Logis* (of which two were French)
— 10 *Brigadiers* (of which two were French)
— 2 Blacksmiths
— 85 Troopers

In 1807, the following were added to their strength:
— Training Captain
— 1 Second-Lieutenant Guidon-Bearer
— 4 Tail-Bearer
— 1 Brigadier Trumpeter
— 2 Trumpeters

Equipment

This was black, red green or white (mostly during campaigns) and comprised a cartridge pouch belt, carbine holder belt, a kubur (a sheath for two pistols) and a sabre cord.

Armament

These were especially made by the Versailles Manufacture. It comprised a blunderbuss (only used on parades), a carbine, two "saddle" pistols, two "side" pistols, one "oriental-style" sabre, one dagger, a mace and an axe.

Harnesses

These were "oriental-style". The saddle comprised very high half-moon-shaped cantles and pommels. It was covered with a green cloth saddlecloth, with white and crimson braid and fringes.

Emblems

The Mamelukes had a guidon from 1802, but what it looked like is not known. After their unforgettable charge at Austerlitz, Napoleon granted the Mamelukes an Eagle. In May 1813, the squadron received an 1812-model standard. During parades, the standard-bearer was accompanied by four *tougs*. These oriental emblems consisted of a horse tail hanging from a shaft. During the campaigns the Mamelukes carried a pennant to replace their standard.

"ORIENTAL-STYLE" UNIFORMS

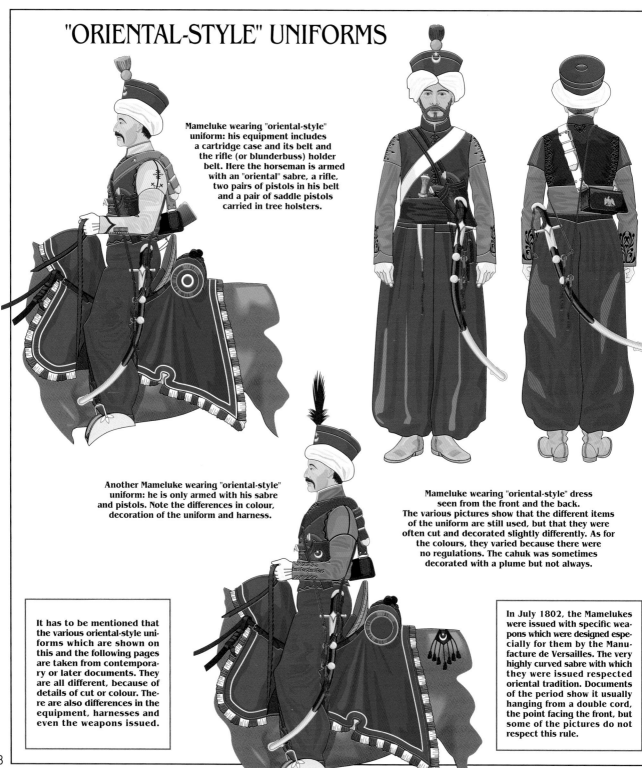

Mameluke wearing "oriental-style" uniform: his equipment includes a cartridge case and its belt and the rifle (or blunderbuss) holder belt. Here the horseman is armed with an "oriental" sabre, a rifle, two pairs of pistols in his belt and a pair of saddle pistols carried in tree holsters.

Another Mameluke wearing "oriental-style" uniform: he is only armed with his sabre and pistols. Note the differences in colour, decoration of the uniform and harness.

Mameluke wearing "oriental-style" dress seen from the front and the back. The various pictures show that the different items of the uniform are still used, but that they were often cut and decorated slightly differently. As for the colours, they varied because there were no regulations. The cahuk was sometimes decorated with a plume but not always.

It has to be mentioned that the various oriental-style uniforms which are shown on this and the following pages are taken from contemporary or later documents. They are all different, because of details of cut or colour. There are also differences in the equipment, harnesses and even the weapons issued.

In July 1802, the Mamelukes were issued with specific weapons which were designed especially for them by the Manufacture de Versailles. The very highly curved sabre with which they were issued respected oriental tradition. Documents of the period show it usually hanging from a double cord, the point facing the front, but some of the pictures do not respect this rule.

"ORIENTAL-STYLE" UNIFORMS

Mameluke wearing oriental-style dress after an engraving by Martinet. Note that the shabrack does not have any fringes but instead it is decorated with an eagle embroidered in the rear angles. Unlike most of the pictures of the period the sabre here is not hanging from a crimson cord but from a black belt with two straps and is carried cutting edge facing downwards. As for the saddle, it is not the normal "oriental" model: it is a classic "Hungarian-style" model but it is however fitted with the special Mameluke stirrups.

"Oriental dress" according to a German engraving by C.G.H. Geissler made in 1806. He bears a *Brigadier's* stripes embroidered in black braid. This engraving is the only one which to our knowledge shows a horseman with the shoulder belts crossed over: the cartridge case is therefore not being worn on the correct side. The shal which surrounds the base of the cahuk is yellow here whereas it should be white as is shown by the majority of engravings of the time.

One could be led to believe that this Mameluke was of eastern descent because of the large amount of decorative embroidery to be seen on the different items of his uniform.

Knives etc., which were issued to the Mamelukes, were very specific. There were four and they were made at the Manufacture de Versailles: an "oriental-style" sabre with a very pronounced curve, a dagger, a mace and an axe.

Another example of a Mameluke wearing "oriental-style" uniform. Note the raised shape of the cantle of the oriental-style saddle used by the Mamelukes. This special harness cost more than that of the *Chasseurs à Cheval.*

9

"ORIENTAL-STYLE" UNIFORMS

Three of the firearms used specifically by the Mamelukes: the blunderbuss used for parades; the pistol carried in saddle holsters and the "side" pistol carried in a sheath attached to the belt.

Mameluke *Brigadier* wearing "oriental-style" uniform. He is wearing the white *sherual*. This drawing was made after a painting by Charlet.

As with knives etc., the firearms were produced by the Manufacture de Versailles and were designed in a style which was harmonised with rest. The carbine that was used during campaigns has not been shown because there is no reliable reproduction in existence. According to Jean Boudriot, the Mamelukes could have been armed with the Infantry 1793-model which was also produced by the Manufacture de Versailles. Moreover the period drawings show that the Mamelukes also used the classic An IX cavalry musketoon with a *tringle*.

Mameluke wearing "oriental-style" dress during the 1813 German Campaign. Note the unusual colour of the schabrack which is blue and not green as usual.

Mameluke NCO wearing "oriental-style" dress. This silhouette was inspired by the sketches and notes made by General Vanson during the ceremony on 15 August during which the veterans of the *Grande Armée* went to lay wreathes at the foot of the *Vendôme* column to celebrate the Emperor's birthday.

10

The "FRENCH" MAMELUKES

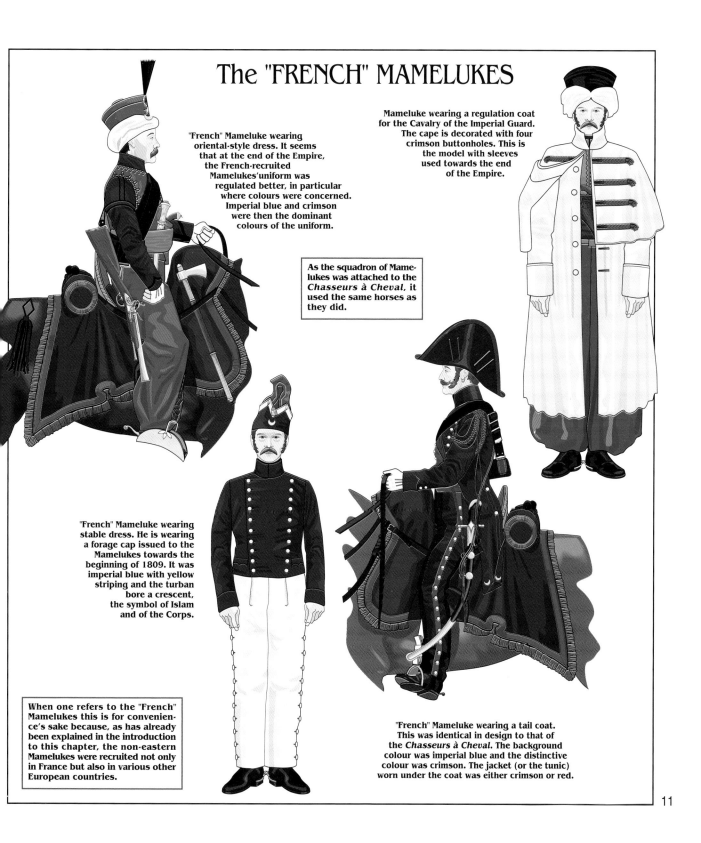

"French" Mameluke wearing oriental-style dress. It seems that at the end of the Empire, the French-recruited Mamelukes'uniform was regulated better, in particular where colours were concerned. Imperial blue and crimson were then the dominant colours of the uniform.

Mameluke wearing a regulation coat for the Cavalry of the Imperial Guard. The cape is decorated with four crimson buttonholes. This is the model with sleeves used towards the end of the Empire.

As the squadron of Mamelukes was attached to the *Chasseurs à Cheval*, it used the same horses as they did.

"French" Mameluke wearing stable dress. He is wearing a forage cap issued to the Mamelukes towards the beginning of 1809. It was imperial blue with yellow striping and the turban bore a crescent, the symbol of Islam and of the Corps.

When one refers to the "French" Mamelukes this is for convenience's sake because, as has already been explained in the introduction to this chapter, the non-eastern Mamelukes were recruited not only in France but also in various other European countries.

"French" Mameluke wearing a tail coat. This was identical in design to that of the *Chasseurs à Cheval*. The background colour was imperial blue and the distinctive colour was crimson. The jacket (or the tunic) worn under the coat was either crimson or red.

"FRENCH-STYLE" UNIFORMS

After 1804, the Mameluke NCOs and officers wore a second "French-style" uniform for indoor town duty. Note that the officers also had a pelisse with gold braid and the NCOs a pelisse with yellow braid. They wore blue breeches with sheepskin with crimson stripes, and a frock coat. The trumpeters also had a "French-style" uniform which was sky blue. As for the ordinary troopers – always supposing that the Mamelukes were issued with a "French-style" uniform – there are no traces of this anywhere in the various inventories, except for the grey riding sheepskin breeches mentioned on page 13.

NCO's frock coat. The officer's coat was cut in the same manner but made of finer cloth. The officers wore their gold aglet on the right or a fringeless epaulette on the left, depending on the regulations applicable to the French Cavalry of the period.

NCO wearing a pelisse and trousers, a uniform which one could call "winter town dress" although this would be without any guarantee of historical exactitude.

Maréchal-des-Logis wearing a coat. As with the *Chasseurs à Cheval* NCOs he is wearing the aglet and the trefoil with mixed gold and crimson which replaced the scarlet. The sabre cord is the same. Note that Raoul and Jean Brunon in their work on the Mamelukes show that the NCO's aglet was a mix of blue and gold.

Maréchal-des-Logis Chef wearing a frock coat and breeches. This was morning quarters uniform.

Subaltern wearing quarters dress.

Subaltern wearing "French-style" uniform.

The MAMELUKE TRUMPETERS

Mameluke trumpeter wearing "oriental dress". At first sight nothing enables the trumpeter to be distinguished from the simple trooper in this uniform, except for the sky blue shirt (*benish*) and the fact that he is riding a white horse.

Mameluke trumpeter wearing "French" uniform. The coat is sky blue. The collar, the lapels and the facings are decorated with braid which seems to be a mix of gold and crimson. The same can be said for the trefoil and the aglet.

Cymbalist.

Mameluke trumpet after one of Commandant Bucquoy's cards.

Mameluke trumpeter wearing quarters or stable dress. He is wearing grey breeches with sheepskin which according to Raoul and Jean Brunon appeared in the depot inventories towards the beginning of 1813. This item was only worn by the second Mamelukes (Young Guard). As for the forage cap, this was the same as the trooper's but with gold and crimson braid.

13

The TIMPANIST

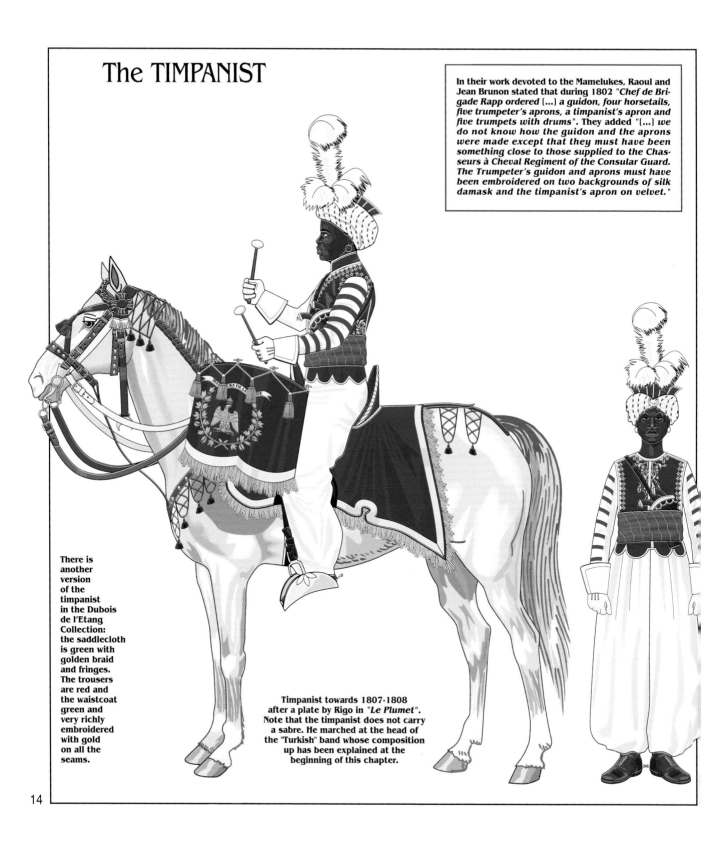

In their work devoted to the Mamelukes, Raoul and Jean Brunon stated that during 1802 "*Chef de Brigade Rapp ordered (...) a guidon, four horsetails, five trumpeter's aprons, a timpanist's apron and five trumpets with drums*". They added "*(...) we do not know how the guidon and the aprons were made except that they must have been something close to those supplied to the Chasseurs à Cheval Regiment of the Consular Guard. The Trumpeter's guidon and aprons must have been embroidered on two backgrounds of silk damask and the timpanist's apron on velvet.*"

There is another version of the timpanist in the Dubois de l'Etang Collection: the saddlecloth is green with golden braid and fringes. The trousers are red and the waistcoat green and very richly embroidered with gold on all the seams.

Timpanist towards 1807-1808 after a plate by Rigo in "*Le Plumet*". Note that the timpanist does not carry a sabre. He marched at the head of the "Turkish" band whose composition up has been explained at the beginning of this chapter.

14

The OFFICERS

Officer's saddle pistol, saddle holster and axe.

Subaltern.
On the rare pictures of Mameluke officers which exist, it is not easy to distinguish the rank insignia among all the embroidery. Only the horseman Kirmann's Squadron Commander's stripes are clearly visible.

Officer's cartridge case. It is made of red leather covered with crimson velvet embroidered with gold.

Belt holster or *koubour*. This sheath was worn saltire-wise and held in place by the sash belt.

Mameluke officer after a gouache by Hoffmann which can be dated from the Consular period, or from the beginning of the Empire.

15

EMBLEMS

The Mamelukes were not given an Eagle with the 5 December 1804 awards. It was granted to them on 15 April 1806 by decree because of their brilliant conduct at Austerlitz. The guidon ordered in 1802 (see p. 14) was then replaced by the 1804 model.

When it returned to the capital on 25 November 1807 after the Prussian and Polish Campaigns, the Guard was awarded 19 laurel wreathes by Frochot, the Prefet of Paris to commemorate the victory at Austerlitz. One of these was fixed to the Mamelukes' Eagle.

Second-Lieutenant Pierre Mérat was appointed the *"Standard-Bearer of the Mamelukes attached to the Guard"* by a decree dated 18 December 1806.

1812-type standard awarded to the Mameluke squadron in May 1813. The standard and its Eagle disappeared in 1814.

This new standard was not carried during the Saxon Campaign. It was probably replaced by an embroidered pennant (see below).

Square pennant measuring 17 1/2 by 17 1/2 inch square. It was made of crimson velvet, the embroidery and the edges were silver. It is not known whether it was surmounted by a point or some other symbol.

Tail-Bearer NCO. The *toug* borrowed from the Turks by the Egyptian Mamelukes was a symbol of authority and war. It was made up of a shaft surmounted by an ornament made of worked copper. A horse tail was attached to the base of this. In order to respect their traditions, the Mamelukes of the Guard were issued with four tougs: one tail was red, one white and the other two black. During parades, they formed up around the guidon, but no text is known which explains how they were placed around the guidon.

The POLISH CHEVAU-LEGERS

Napoleon entered Warsaw in December 1806. A Guard of Honour made up of Polish nobles ensured the Emperor's protection along with the Imperial Guard. Impressed by the escort's uniform, Napoleon decided to incorporate a regiment of Poles into his Guard. It was created by decree, dated 2 March 1807. A decree dated 16 April required that to be admitted into the regiment the candidates had to be "*proprietors or the sons of proprietors, be aged 18 at least and 40 at most, and be able to equip themselves with uniform, equipment, complete harnesses according to the models, etc.*"

As and when the squadrons were formed, they went to France and took up their quarters at Chantilly. The Poles only occupied the barracks for a short time because they left for Spain in February 1808. In April the Emperor inspected them and was not very pleased with their lack of military spirit and the low level of their training. He therefore entrusted them to his aide de camp, General Durosnel, for him to complete their training. This training was finished off by Lasalle who taught them front-line service and turned them into a real cavalry regiment.

When they returned from training in November 1808, the Polish Chevau-Légers had the opportunity to show their mettle very quickly. On the 30th of the same month following a direct order from the Emperor, at Somo-Sierra, the 3rd Squadron of Poles, only 150-men strong, attacked 9 000 infantry entrenched on the slopes near the road, and the batteries of four artillery pieces installed on each of the four bends. The charge lasted seven minutes during which the Chevau-Légers knocked out four batteries, put the enemy to flight and took a flag for the loss of 83 men and 7 officers, killed or wounded. They were now worthy of being part of the Guard.

In the spring of 1809, the regiment returned to France and set off almost immediately for Austria. At Wagram, the Poles charged the Uhlans under Schwarzenberg and captured their lances and used them against their original owners. This "war booty" changed the destiny of the unit. The regiment adopted the lance as its principal weapon in December 1809 and the Chevau-Légers became the Chevau-légers lancers.

In January of 1810, two squadrons left for Spain. In June 1812, the Chevau-Légers Lancers were on the banks of the Niemen, ready to invade Russia. In August they fought at Smolensk, in September at the Moskova (Borodino), and then entered Moscow. Out of the 1 109 horsemen who had left barely six months earlier, only 185 returned to France at the end of the terrible retreat from Russia.

The Emperor's Poles fought in Germany in 1813, and then crossed back over the Rhine at the beginning of 1814 to take part gloriously in the French Campaign. They fought at Brienne, La Rothière, Champaubert, Vauchamp, Montereau. After the Emperor abdicated, a detachment of 109 horsemen accompanied Napoleon to Elba. The rest of the regiment under the command of General Krasinski, presented themselves to Grand Duke Constantine and returned to Poland.

When the Guard was reorganised during the Hundred Days, the Poles who were too few to form a 1st Regiment, were amalgamated into the 2nd Regiment of Chevau-Légers of the Guard – the Red Lancers – and took the position of 1st Squadron under the orders of General de Colbert. They won a final battle at Ligny, and charged at Waterloo.

The decree setting up the regiment stipulated that it should consist of 4 two-squadron companies. On 11 March a fifth squadron was created which brought the strength up to 1 500 men. On 11 April 1813 a sixth squadron was raised. The result of this was to split the regiment into three squadrons of Old Guard and three of Young Guard. In July 1813, a seventh squadron of Young Guard was created (see the chapter on 3rd Regiment of Chevau-Légers Lancers of the Guard.) In December of the same year, the strength was reduced to four squadrons. Finally the squadron, which survived all this turmoil, comprised 120 horsemen and took part in the Belgian Campaign in 1815.

Uniforms

These were of Polish origin. The Polish names designating the different items were Frenchified by the Imperial administration but the spelling varied according to the different transcriptions. Only the most characteristics of these items will be described here.

The shapska came directly from the Polish national head dress, a cap with a square top. Its shape and decoration remained unchanged throughout the Empire. Only its height was reduced by one inch. It comprised a crown made of crimson cloth, with a leather crown with a visor and a chain chinstrap. It had white braid and all the metal decorations were silver, except for the spokes/grooves of the front plate and the crowned "N". It bore a tricolour cockade covered with a silver Maltese cross. When worn on parade, it had a white plume and a double cord made of white thread with tassels and flounders.

The kurtka was made of dark blue cloth, slightly paler than imperial blue. The collar, lapels, facings, turnbacks and piping were all crimson; the buttons were made of brass. The lapels were edged with 5/8-inch wide silver braid. It had an aglet, finished with silver tags, and one epaulette, both of which were made of white thread.

The blue uniform trousers had a double crimson stripe down both sides; the bottoms of the legs were very tight-fitting, opening halfway up the side of the calf. This was fastened by five crimson cord laces.

Apart from this uniform, the Chevau-Légers were issued with marching trousers, a single coloured sleeveless waistcoat, a stable waistcoat, fatigues, a coat, small boots, a forage cap and a saddle-pack. These uniform items remained the same during the whole Empire; only the coat was changed: sleeves were added.

Weapons

Weapons included a sabre, a musketoon with its bayonet and a pistol. When the regiment was created, the weapons were Prussian; when they returned to France, the Chevau-Légers were issued with An XI-model sabres with metals scabbards, An IX-model musketoons and An IX or An XIII-model pistols. The An XI-model sabre was soon replaced by that used by the Chasseurs of the Guard. In December 1809, the Chevau-Légers were issued with a lance.

Equipment

The straps made of whitened buffalo hide were stitched as they were in the other corps of the Guard. The cartridge-pouch belt, the musketoon-holder belt, the platine cover and the sabre-knot were identical to those of the Chasseurs à Cheval.

Harnesses

These were the classic "Hungarian-style" harnesses as used throughout all the Light cavalry. The shabrack was dark blue and edged with crimson piping and crimson braid with white filet. It was decorated with a white thread eagle in the rear corners and a crowned "N" in the front ones. The accessories were made of black leather and of Hungarian leather.

The Buglers

They were dressed like the troopers but the background colour of their uniform evolved during the course of the Empire. When the regiment was formed, the background colour was crimson with white distinctives; from 1810 onwards, it was white with crimson distinctives and silver braid; this remained unchanged until the end. The service dress was dark sky blue with crimson distinctives, colours which were attributed to all the trumpeters of the cavalry of the Guard. A trumpeter fitted out with a particularly sumptuous uniform and equipment had the job of timpanist.

The Officers

Normally the uniform worn by the officers was the same as that of the troopers, but it was made out of finer cloth and all the trimmings were silver. Indeed the officers had a number of extra items and in the case of the Chevau-Légers, they were varied and quite luxurious. This is the list given according to Lucien Rousselot: *"Two or three kurtkas, two or three pairs of trousers, two tail coats, an overcoat, a frock coat, waistcoats, short breeches, one pair of Hungarian-style breeches, and a greatcoat to which were added the headdress, equipment, weapons and harnesses..."* It is impossible in the context of this book to describe in detail all the different uniforms and their accessories: it is worth consulting Plate N°75 which Lucien Rousselot devoted to the officers of the Chevau-Légers.

The REGIMENT in 1807

It consisted of four squadrons with two companies each and a headquarters.

Headquarters:
— 1 Colonel Commanding
— 2 French Majors
— 4 Squadron Commanders
— 1 Quartermaster-Treasurer
— 1 French Instructor Captain
— 2 French *Adjudant-Majors*
— 4 *Sous-Adjudant-Majors* taken from the Polish regiments which had served in France
— 1 Eagle-Bearer
— 4 Health Officers
— 1 *Maréchal-des-Logis Chef* Assistant Instructor
— 1 Veterinary Artist and 2 Aides
— 1 Trumpet-Major
— 2 *Brigadiers-Trompettes*
— 1 Master-Tailor
— 1 Master-Breech-maker
— 1 Master-Armourer
— 1 Master-Boot-maker
— 1 Master-Saddler
— 1 Master Spur-Maker
— 2 Blacksmiths

The men were assigned to each of the **8 companies** as follows:

— 1 Captain
— 2 First-Lieutenants
— 2 Second-Lieutenants
— 1 *Maréchal-des-Logis Chef*
— 6 *Maréchaux des Logis*
— 1 *Fourrier*
— 10 *Brigadiers*
— 97 Troopers
— 3 Trumpeters
— 2 Blacksmiths

FULL DRESS

Uniform worn when the regiment
was first created in 1807, after a gouache
by Lucien Rousselot. Note two details which
were characteristic of this uniform: first the
plaited cord worn in the normal way as on
a shako which was replaced by a simple
cord made of white thread, rolled around
the crown of the shapska. Note however that
certain period documents prove that the
plaited cord continued to be worn sometimes
as late as 1813. The second detail is the
slanted design of the turnback pockets. This
was modified subsequently. When they were
created in March 1807, the Chevau-Légers
received poor quality Prussian-made sabres.
It was only after 1809 that they were
armed with the Light Cavalry
An XI-model sabre.

Polish Chevau-Léger
wearing full dress, after
an engraving by Martinet.
This picture could logically
be dated 1807-1809 since
this man is still wearing the
plaited cord on his shapska
and the aglet on his right.
Note the strange ornaments
on the lapels and the fact
that he is wearing
two epaulettes
instead of one.

Mounted
full dress
before
the lance
was adopted.
The aglet
is worn on
the right.
The
musketoon
is carried
in the normal
way, i.e. on
the right-hand
side. The sabre
is the Light
Cavalry of the
Line model.

19

FULL DRESS

A Polish Chevau-Léger Lancer according to the Dresden Camp Manuscript illustrated by Sauerweid (1813). This horseman is still wearing the cord of the shapska like that of a shako, a practice which had been abandoned by the regiment a long time before. He has a pair of epaulettes moreover and strangely enough his belt plate does not have any design on it. It can be presumed that the rank stripes are actually hidden by the gauntlets; the collar stripe would thus seem to indicate that the man is a *brigadier*.

When the lance was adopted in December 1809, the Chevau-Légers, who had become Lancers in the meantime, nevertheless kept the sabre, pistol and musketoon with its bayonet. It was with this heavy load of weapons that they left for Russia in 1812. The lessons learnt from this disastrous campaign showed that the men in the second rank did not need a lance. As a result, in April 1813, the weapons were spread out more evenly: in each company, the front rank was armed with a lance, a sabre and a pistol. The *Maréchal-de-Logis* were armed with a sabre and two pistols; only four *Brigadiers* carried the full armament. The second rank including the *Brigadiers* was armed with a sabre, a pistol and a musketoon.

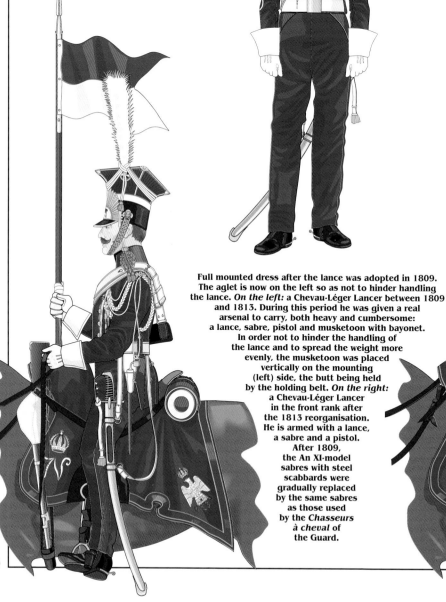

Full mounted dress after the lance was adopted in 1809. The aglet is now on the left so as not to hinder handling the lance. *On the left:* a Chevau-Léger Lancer between 1809 and 1813. During this period he was given a real arsenal to carry, both heavy and cumbersome: a lance, sabre, pistol and musketoon with bayonet. In order not to hinder the handling of the lance and to spread the weight more evenly, the musketoon was placed vertically on the mounting (left) side, the butt being held by the holding belt. *On the right:* a Chevau-Léger Lancer in the front rank after the 1813 reorganisation. He is armed with a lance, a sabre and a pistol. After 1809, the An XI-model sabres with steel scabbards were gradually replaced by the same sabres as those used by the *Chasseurs à cheval* of the Guard.

CAMPAIGN DRESS

Chevau-Léger Lancer wearing stable dress. This comprises a waistcoat with sleeves and canvas trousers worn in the billets during the summer months (after a drawing by P. Benigni).

One of the lightweight campaign uniforms, according to a drawing by P. Benigni, worn in Spain in 1808 on the recommendation of Major Dautancourt. In fact this consisted of the stable dress with full equipment and the shapska, in its oilskin cover.

Chevau-Léger Lancer wearing a greatcoat. The first greatcoat issued to the Polish Chevau-Légers was ample, without sleeves or round-cloak. When the lance was adopted, they were issued with a greatcoat with round-cloak and with sleeves which was more practical when handling this cumbersome weapon.

Chevau-Léger Lancer wearing campaign uniform, 1810-1812. As was the case when travelling, the troopers always unbuttoned the right-hand lapel and buttoned it across on the left which allowed the crimson edging on this side to be seen. Note also the way that the corners of the saddle cloth have been turned up and attached to the holding belt.

CAMPAIGN DRESS

Chevau-Léger Lancer wearing the uniform worn
during the German and the French campaigns
in 1813 and 1814. The pennant on the lance when
the ordinary marching uniform was worn remained
rolled around the lance shaft and was protected
by an oilcloth sheath. The greatcoat was carried
saltire-wise, a position which could be adopted
en route but which was used especially
at the moment the troopers charged.

Uniform worn
during the French
Campaign (1814).
This is a Brigadier
who is recognisable
by his rank stripe.
His rather wide
travelling trousers
do not have any side
openings nor do
they have any
leather covering
the crotch.
The bottoms
of the legs
have false
boots.

Chevau-Léger and Chevau-Léger Lancer wearing campaign dress.
They are wearing travelling trousers which were ampler than
the uniform trousers. They had a strip of crimson cloth
with buttonholes down the sides. Leather reinforcements
were sewn onto the right thigh to protect the cloth
from being worn through by the musketoon
when it was carried on that side.

CLOTHING

Shapska cockade.

Trooper's shapska.

Shapska cockade worn by the squadron which accompanied Napoleon to Elba.

NCO's shapska.

Polish Chevau-Léger's kurtka. Silver lapel stripe. Epaulette in white thread lined with crimson cloth. Aglet made of white thread mounted in a trefoil, lined with crimson cloth. Silver tags.

Brigadier's **kurtka. It has a silver stripe above the facing and on the collar.**

1/2 bell button.

Shirt.

Fourrier's kurtka: the aglet and the epaulette were the same as for the *Maréchal-des-Logis.*

Maréchal-des-Logis' kurtka. Unlike his French counterpart, the Polish *Maréchal-des-Logis* wore two stripes above the facings; the aglet and the epaulette were 1/3 silver and 2/3 crimson. The epaulette edging was crimson.

Maréchal-des-Logis Chef' kurtka. He has three silver stripes above the facing; the aglet and epaulette were a mix of 2/3 silver and 1/3 crimson. The epaulette has a silver edging.

The waistcoat worn under the kurtka.

Forage cap with a crimson headband, with white braid for the troopers *(left)* and with silver braid for the NCOs *(right)*.

Detail of the crimson cord lacing which fastened the bottom of the legs of the uniform trousers.

Small boots. With the tight-fitting trousers, it was impossible to wear higher boots.

Travelling trousers.

ARMAMENT and EQUIPMENT

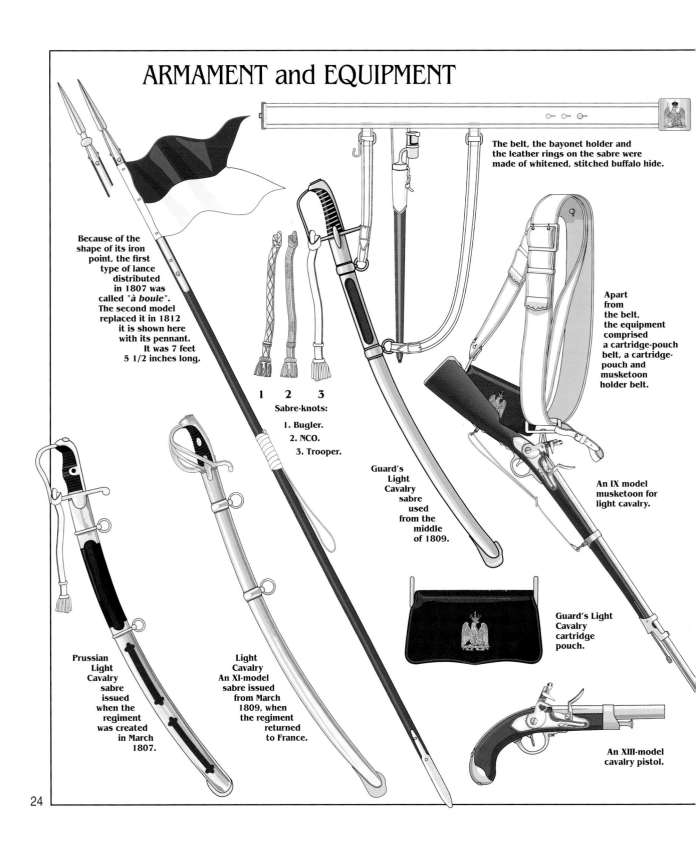

Because of the shape of its iron point, the first type of lance distributed in 1807 was called "*à boule*". The second model replaced it in 1812 it is shown here with its pennant. It was 7 feet 5 1/2 inches long.

The belt, the bayonet holder and the leather rings on the sabre were made of whitened, stitched buffalo hide.

Apart from the belt, the equipment comprised a cartridge-pouch belt, a cartridge-pouch and musketoon holder belt.

1 2 3

Sabre-knots:

1. Bugler.
2. NCO.
3. Trooper.

Guard's Light Cavalry sabre used from the middle of 1809.

An IX model musketoon for light cavalry.

Prussian Light Cavalry sabre issued when the regiment was created in March 1807.

Light Cavalry An XI-model sabre issued from March 1809, when the regiment returned to France.

Guard's Light Cavalry cartridge pouch.

An XIII-model cavalry pistol.

24

SADDLES

Complete Chevau-Léger Lancer saddle and harness. The saddlecloth was made of blue cloth, edged with crimson piping. It had a crimson 2 1/8th-inch braid bordered by two white fillets. Eagles and crowned "N"s embroidered with white thread. The musketoon-holder boot has not been shown here; it was placed either on the offside (right-hand) if the trooper was a Chevau-Léger or on the mount side (left) if he was a Chevau-Léger Lancer.

Complete saddle and harness for trumpeter in full dress. The crimson saddlecloth had white thread braid and was also used for service dress.

When the lance was adopted, the stirrup was fitted with a lance-holder boot fastened with leather laces.

When travelling or campaigning, the trumpeters used the same saddlecloth as the troopers.

According to a custom in the Cavalry, it seems that the inside braid on the Major's saddlecloth (the regiment's second-in-command) was gold in order to match the metal on the top of his epaulettes.

A drawing by Hesse made in the Dresden Camp shows the senior officer here with a saddlecloth with a crimson background.

Saddle and harness belonging to a subaltern. The saddlecloth had braid silver, woven with 2 1/8th-inch stripes. The senior officers' saddlecloths had a second 4/5th-inch braid stripe sewn inside the first.

Detail of the braiding on the senior officer's saddlecloth.

The NCOs

Master-Worker wearing town dress after a plate by Lucien Rousselot. As they had NCO rank the Master-Workers often wore the same style of society and town dress as the officers, but with the distinctives of their rank: the epaulette and the aglet were a mix of crimson and silver, as were the stripe and the trefoils of the "Hungarian-style" breeches. On the other hand, they did not wear any silver braid over the facings.

Maréchal-des-Logis wearing full dress, pre-December 1809.

Maréchal-des-Logis in ordinary uniform after December 1809. After the lance was adopted, the aglet changed sides, from the right to the left, including for NCOs.

Maréchal-des-Logis wearing campaign dress, 1810-1812.

Maréchal-des-Logis in full dress, 1810-1812. He was armed with a sabre and two pistols. The shapska cord and the aglet were a mix of 1/3 silver and 2/3 crimson.

TRUMPETERS

Marching uniform, 1807-1810. The kurtka lapel was crossed over onto the aglet side and revealed the white border. The travelling trousers were those of the troopers.

The trumpet cord was the same for the NCOs and the simple buglers.

From 1807-1810, the cord for the full dress uniform trumpets was made of white thread mixed with 1/3 silver. Those for the service dress were similar, but the proportion of silver was smaller.

All the metal decorations on the first shapskas which were made in Poland were brass. Where the crown joined the turban was covered with 3/4 inch braid comprising a silver stripe edged with two white-thread stripes.

After 1808, all the decorations on the shapskas made in France were silver except for the bands on the plate and the imperial emblem which was made of brass. The braid which covered where the crown joined the turban was completely silver; it was an inch wide. On Plate N° 47, Lucien Rousselot showed that the kurtkas of the first bugler uniform did not have decorated buttonholes; but another of his plates preserved in the Anne S.K. Brown Collection seems to prove the opposite. It is this one which has been shown here.

Buglers in full dress, 1807-1810.

When the regiment was formed, the buglers wore a kurtka made of crimson cloth with white collar, facings, lapels and turnbacks, edged with 5/8 inch-wide silver braid. The trousers were crimson with a double white stripe and white piping between them. All the trimmings were a mix of white and silver: the aglet, the epaulette, the shapska cord, the trumpet cord and the sabre knot. The epaulette loops were made of 3/8 inch-wide silver braid. The plume was entirely white. At the beginning, the buglers probably used the same saddlecloth as the troopers; then they were given a full dress shabrack made of crimson cloth. They nevertheless kept the troopers' shabrack for the marching and ordinary service dress.

TRUMPETERS

Trumpet-Major wearing parade uniform, 1810-1814. He is recognisable by the three *Maréchal-des-Logis-Chef* stripes on his sleeves and the second stripe on his collar. Being assigned to headquarters, he wore a white plume.

From 1810, the trumpet cords on the ordinary service dress were made of crimson thread mixed with silver.

Trumpeter wearing parade dress, 1810-1814.

The parade belt and cartridge box were covered in crimson cloth on which three silver stripes were sewn a regular intervals. They revealed the background cloth in the gaps between them and on the two sides. All the metal parts of the equipment were made of brass.

Reverse side of the trumpet apron of the parade dress. It was also called "*étendard*".

According to Lucien Rousselot, the new uniform was probably made in the irst months of 1810, in anticipation of the festivities for the wedding of Napoleon and Marie-Louise. The kurtka was now white but the crimson trousers with white stripes were kept, as was the saddlecloth and the saddle-pack.

TRUMPETER'S CLOTHING

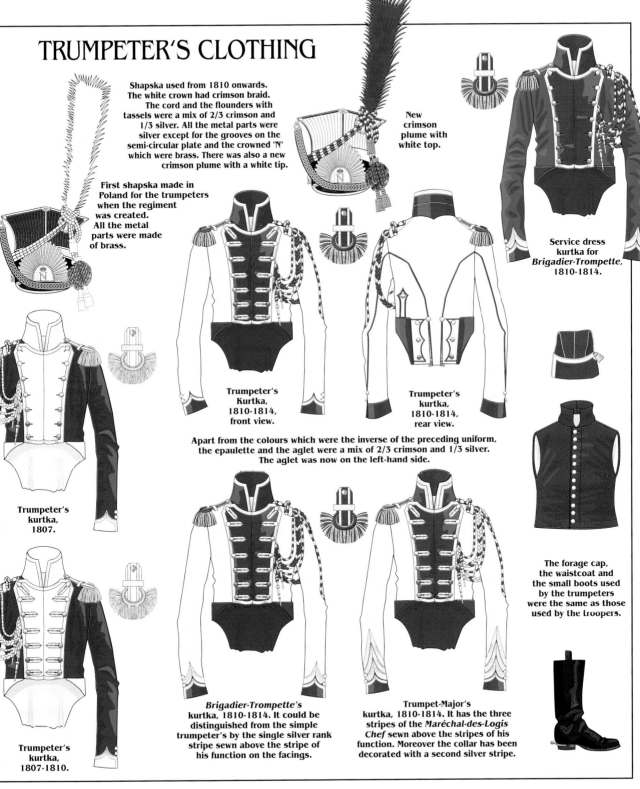

Shapska used from 1810 onwards. The white crown had crimson braid. The cord and the flounders with tassels were a mix of 2/3 crimson and 1/3 silver. All the metal parts were silver except for the grooves on the semi-circular plate and the crowned "N" which were brass. There was also a new crimson plume with a white tip.

First shapska made in Poland for the trumpeters when the regiment was created. All the metal parts were made of brass.

New crimson plume with white top.

Service dress kurtka for *Brigadier-Trompette*, 1810-1814.

Trumpeter's Kurtka, 1810-1814, front view.

Trumpeter's kurtka, 1810-1814, rear view.

Apart from the colours which were the inverse of the preceding uniform, the epaulette and the aglet were a mix of 2/3 crimson and 1/3 silver. The aglet was now on the left-hand side.

Trumpeter's kurtka, 1807.

Trumpeter's kurtka, 1807-1810.

Brigadier-Trompette's kurtka, 1810-1814. It could be distinguished from the simple trumpeter's by the single silver rank stripe sewn above the stripe of his function on the facings.

Trumpet-Major's kurtka, 1810-1814. It has the three stripes of the *Maréchal-des-Logis Chef* sewn above the stripes of his function. Moreover the collar has been decorated with a second silver stripe.

The forage cap, the waistcoat and the small boots used by the trumpeters were the same as those used by the troopers.

29

The TIMPANIST

The Polish headdress was a sort of very richly decorated *"confederatka"* consisting of a crown embroidered with gold, a fur turban above which there was golden braid embellished with precious stones (jade or turquoise), a cord with golden flounders, a white aigrette, and crimson and white feathers.

The head harness comprised a 17th Century oriental bridle. It was covered with golden scales decorated with precious stones. The reins were made of gold braid. A crimson and white plume was placed above the head and the front was decorated with gold and crimson tassels. The breast strap (invisible here) was covered with the same golden scales as the bridle. It was decorated with three golden tassels.

Polish Chevau-Léger Timpanist of the Guard wearing full parade dress, 1810, after Martinet.

The uniform was made up of a gold embroidered crimson corselet together with a white sleeveless tunic; a wide crimson sash with golden fringes; baggy sky-blue trousers with gold braid; tawny leather boots. The timpanist was armed with an "oriental-style" sabre hanging from a crimson thread baldric.

CHEVAU-LÉGERS POLONAIS

The timpanist in the Polish Chevau-Légers was French. Born in Lille on 15 February 1787, Jean-Louis Robiquet entered the regiment as a trumpeter on 1 February 1808. He took part in the Spanish Campaign in the same year, and in the German one in 1809. On 1 July 1810, Major Dautancourt chose him from among the other trumpeters to become a timpanist probably, according to Lucien Rousselot, because he was small (5 ft 4 in). He was then attached to the headquarters. In June 1812, he left with his regiment for the Russian Campaign. He disappeared at Borissov during the retreat of sad memory. There are no documents enabling us to ascertain whether or not he was replaced by another trumpeter after his death.

SADDLE and TIMPANI APRONS

According to Lucien Rousselot, the saddle cover measured 5 ft 8 in along its lower edge, 4 ft 3 in across the middle, 5 ft 8 in across the withers and 5 ft 3 in at the rear corners. It was made of crimson velvet, fringed with big cable stitching and entirely embroidered with golden thread. The oriental saddle was also covered with crimson velvet embroidered with gold.

The timpani apron measured 3 ft 11 in long and 1 ft 10 in high. They were made of crimson velvet with gold braid and fringes. The decoration consisted of foliage and small palms, four Lictors' fasces and a laurel wreath crown surrounding an eagle. Four crowns decorated the corners. The bottom of the apron had twenty-eight silver stars. The whole was mounted with a silver band of ribbon on which the inscription "CHEVAU-LEGERS POLONAIS" was embroidered with black thread.

CHEVAU-LEGERS POLONAIS

TRUMPETER'S CAMPAIGN DRESS

Brigadier-Trompette in marching uniform, 1810-1814.

Obverse and reverse side of a trumpet standard attributed to the Chevau-Légers.

This item was published in *La Giberne*, 12th Year and taken up by Lucien Rousselot in his plate N°65.

Probably adopted for parades towards 1808, this would have been kept for ordinary service dress.

Trumpeter according to the Dresden Camp Manuscript, about 1813.

Trumpeter wearing ordinary service dress, 1810-1814.

Trumpeter wearing Guard Duty uniform, 1810-1814.

Trumpeter in campaign dress, about 1814.

OFFICER'S FULL DRESS

The collar, the lapels, the facings and the turnbacks on the full dress kurtka were edged with the same silver embroidery for all ranks, but the width varied according to each officer's taste and purse. The buttons were silver. The trousers were the same as the troopers' but the double crimson stripe was generally wider. There were also crimson parade trousers, with white side stripes. The crown of the shapska was covered with crimson cloth; it was also fluted and stitched. All the metal parts were silver except for the grooves of the plate and the crowned "N" which were made of golden brass. Where the turban joined the crown there was 2 $^{1/8}$ inch-wide silver braid for subalterns, and a 2 $^{1/8}$ – 2 $^{1/2}$ inch-wide strip of crimson cloth embroidered with silver oak and laurel leaves for senior officers. The cord, folded double, was wound twice round the crown. It had silver trimmings and was finished with flounders and fringed tassels. The officers used two belts: a broad one with a silver buckle decorated with a silver eagle and a narrow one with a hooked "s" clasp. Both of them were made of silver cloth mounted on red morocco; the buckles were silver. In full dress the officers wore a sash, 6 feet long by 19 $^{1/2}$ in wide with silver thread and light crimson silk thread; with two fringed tassels with silver trimming.

Subaltern in service dress, 1807-1814.

Subaltern in parade dress, 1807-1814.

The uniform belonging to General Krasinski, the Colonel commanding the regiment. As was the custom in the Guard, he held the rank of Major-General. On the kurtka of officers of senior rank, the usual embroidery was replaced by oak leaves with serrated beading.

Cartridge box with a body made of black leather with a silver flap circled with cane and decorated with an eagle placed on a radiant sun, the whole made of golden metal. The sides of the box were decorated with golden lion's heads. The belt was made of silver cloth mounted on red morocco. The metal decorations were silver and golden. This is not the only model: there were different variations.

OFFICER'S CAMPAIGN DRESS

When the officers wore service dress for marching or campaigning, luxury was quite out of place. The kurtka lapels were folded over to protect the embroidery; the shapska had an oilcloth sheath; the strap and the flap of the cartridge case had leather sheathes fastened with buttons. The silver cloth belts were replaced by a white buffalo hide belt. Moreover they wore less tightly-fitting trousers which had reinforcements between the legs and no lacings. They wore a service dress kurtka on which there was embroidery only on the collar, the facings and the turnbacks. The lapels were blue, edged with crimson but without embroidery.

Officer in full service dress. He is wearing the Gold Cross of the 4th Class of the Military Order of the Duchy of Warsaw.

Officer at the Battle of the Moskova in September 1812, after a period aquarelle taken up by P. Benigni. Note the "à la Lasalle" trousers which Lucien Rousselot considered as being probably an exception.

Officer wearing a cape-coat.

Officer wearing campaign dress.

Officer wearing campaign dress.

34

OFFICER'S TOWN and SOCIAL DRESS

Subaltern wearing town dress, 1810-1814.

Subaltern wearing an overcoat, 1810-1814.

When wearing service dress, the officers wore a soft cap called a "*konfederatka*". Its top was square and was made of crimson cloth without fluting. The turban was made of astrakhan edged with silver braid or embroidered crimson braid.

Subaltern wearing a frock coat, 1810-1814.

Subaltern wearing social dress, 1807-1808.

Subaltern wearing social dress, 1810-1814.

Subaltern wearing gala uniform, 1810-1814.

OFFICER'S PARADE DRESS

The silver thread and light crimson silk sash worn by officers in full dress.

The white kurtka used for full parade dress was to have been used by all officers when the regiment was created. It was to have been made in France, but the regiment started campaigning only a few months after it was formed and this prevented the items being made. Lucien Rousselot thinks that it was used by only a few senior officers and then in exceptional circumstances. According to period iconography, there were even two models: one with decorations on the lapel buttonholes and the other without.

OFFICER'S CLOTHING

Officer's shapska cockade.

Officer's "à la chasseur" sabre derived from the An XI-model.

Embroidered or silver thread sabre-knot with twisted or threaded fringes depending on rank.

Two examples among many others of cartridge cases worn by Chevau-Léger Officers. Above: the second uniform cartridge case body. Opposite: Cartridge case and shoulder belt for full dress both covered with crimson velvet. This ensemble is preserved in the Musée de l'Armée in Paris.

Officer's shapska.

Senior (rank of Major-General) officer's kurtka. The regimental embroidery has been replaced by oak leaves surrounded by a indented strip.

Full dress kurtka, front view, 1807-1814.

Detail of the embroidery decorating the officer's kurtka, whatever his rank.

Full dress kurtka, rear view, 1807-1814.

Overcoat worn with quarters dress.

"A la chasseur" coats used with town and social dress.

Coats worn with ball dress.

EMBLEMS

1804-model standard.

1812-model standard.

Eagle-Bearer Officer
wearing parade dress
towards 1810.

CHEVAU-LÉGERS
POLONAIS

ESCADRON
NAPOLÉON

Chevau-Légers pennant used
by the Island of Elba
Squadron.

The colours and the
symbolism were set
by Napoleon himself.

Lance
pennant
with an
inscription
in Polish.

The 2ⁿᵈ CHEVAU-LEGERS LANCERS

Louis, Napoleon's brother, left his Dutch throne and abdicated on 1 July 1810. On the 9th of the same month, Napoleon united Holland to the Empire and to honour the Dutch army which had served courageously during the 1806 and 1807 Campaigns, he allowed the troops of his brother's exguard into his own Guard.

On 31 July, the Emperor sent the Royal Dutch Guard to France, including the Hussar Regiment, which reached Versailles on 31 august and settled themselves in.

At St-Cloud Palace, on 13 September 1810

"(...) Article 3: The Hussar Regiment in the Dutch Guard will adopt the name of 2ⁿᵈ Regiment of Chevau-Légers Lancers of our own Guard. It will be armed with lances and be composed of eight companies (...) Article 8: The uniform will remain the same, except that the buttons will be replaced by the buttons of our Guard and the frogging will be removed. Article : Eagles will be given to this new part of our Guard."

The organisation of the new regiment started on 21 September supervised by Maréchal Bessières. On 27 November, an instructor and eight NCOs were assigned to Chantilly for six weeks where the Polish lancers were stationed to learn how to handle a lance.

During this period, the new Chevau-Légers Lancers wore their old Dutch Hussar service dress then at the beginning of 1811, they were temporarily given a new "*à la Chasseur*" uniform. It was temporarily indeed because General Edouard de Colbert who was appointed Colonel Commanding the regiment on 6 march 1811 thought that the Chevau-Légers Lancers of the 2ⁿᵈ Regiment should wear a similar uniform to that of the Poles in the 1ˢᵗ Regiment., since they were organised in the same way.

After concerting with the Ministry, a decree dated 10 February 1811 in theory settled the final aspect of the regiment. "*Article 1: the 2ⁿᵈ Regiment of Chevau-légers Lancers of our Guard will wear the same cut of clothes and headdress as the 1ˢᵗ Regiment. It will keep the same scarlet background colour for the coat, with yellow buttons and distinctives. The distinctive colour of lapels, collars and facings will be sky blue.*"

Several tests were made, there were hesitations... It was just that the shapska and the kurtka which were traditional elements of the Polish uniform did not exactly look Dutch... Moreover, the sky blue distinctive was considered to get dirty too easily, so dark blue was tried. Lieutenant Sous-Adjudant major Fallot, called the "Bear" because of his size, height and very hairy chest was the "model". After making his decision, de Colbert made him put on the new "*à la Polonaise*" uniform and presented him to the Emperor who was satisfied and agreed. The marvellous uniform, brand new, was worn for the first time on the 15 August 1811 parade, the Emperor's birthday.

But adopting the new uniform was not without causing serious financial problems for the officers. This was the third time that they had had to change uniform and some to them were heavily in debt with all these purchases. De Colbert had to ask for help of between 1 000 to 1 200 francs for each officer. The Emperor accepted in August 1811: nothing was too good for his Guard; all the more so that the new "Red Lancers" were going to be part of the escort party which was to accompany the imperial couple during its visit to Holland in September.

For sixteen months the new regiment had a garrison life: exercises, escorts, parades. Everything changed on 9 February 1812 at evening roll call: the Lancers who had been on a war footing for several weeks now were given the order to be ready to leave at midnight for a destination known only to the officers. The Russian Campaign had just started... They were going to fight a vanguard war with their Polish brothers-in-arms and were constantly confronted with the Cossacks. They were present at the Moskova, they fought at the Berezina and finished the campaign after losing 633 men. Only 174 escape the Russian hell, and in what state!

The regiment was reformed at the beginning of 1813. It took part in most of the battles of the Saxony Campaign: Lützen, Bautzen, Reichenbach, Dresden, Toeplitz and Leipzig. The Lancers crossed the Rhine on 5 November 1813 and although barely reorganised, set off again in January 1814 to take part in the French Campaign. In May 1814, after the First Abdication, the regiment was reorganised with the squadrons of the Young Guard under the name "*Corps Royal des Chevau-Légers de France*".

Disbanded by decree on 8 April 1815, the unit was immediately reformed with 5 squadrons under the name of "*Régiment des Chevau-Légers Lanciers de la Garde Impériale*". The Polish Chevau-Légers who had followed Napoleon to Elba were incorporated in this unit with the position of 1ˢᵗ Squadron. But Napoleon changed his mind about this a few days later: although remaining incorporated in the regiment, the Poles formed a special unit called the "Polish Squadron". It was again under the command of General de Colbert that the regiment took part in the Belgian Campaign and that it made its last charges at Waterloo.

After the Emperor abdicated on 21 June, the regiment was 39

sent to the Loire and dismissed squadron by squadron between 9 November and 22 December 1815.

Composition

On the review of 18 September 1810, the theoretical strength of the regiment, which had arrived from Holland, was 58 officers and 865 troopers, 1 Trumpet-major and 15 Trumpeters. Organised on 21 September 1810, the make-up was fixed as follows: 1 headquarters and four 2-company squadrons, a total of 58 officers and 881 men, including 1 Trumpet-Major, 2 *Brigadier-Trompettes* and 21 Trumpeters, all of whom were Dutch. The total strength was not reached immediately and was made up gradually: in July 1811, the Emperor decided to assign all the new Velite horsemen of the Guard to the Red Lancers; in December 1811, as there were still 60 men missing, more Velites were recruited.

On 11 March 1812, a 5ᵗʰ two-company squadron was created by decree using various light cavalry regiments of the Line and some Dragoons. As full strength was still not reached, it was made up with some men from some of the former Dutch Hussar regiments which were serving in Spain. The 2ⁿᵈ Chevau-Légers Lancers was part of the Middle Guard except for the officers who were from the Old Guard. On 1 September 1812, the total strength was 1 406 men including 48 Velites. The losses suffered during the Russian Campaign meant that it was necessary to reorganise the regiment completely. Most of the Dutch who had made up the regiment had disappeared and it was decided to use Frenchmen to replace them. On 18 January 1813, the regiment was reorganised into 8 squadrons with 250 men. A new decree dated 12 March stipulated that the first 5 squadrons were to be from the Old Guard and the five new ones were from the Young Guard.

On 12 May 1814, the regiment, renamed "*Corps Royal des Chevau-Légers de France*", was again reorganised into 4 two-company squadrons, totalling 42 officers and 601 men. The new unit was made up of the squadrons of the Young Guard. On 22 April 1815, an imperial decree raised the number of squadrons to 5 and the regiment took back its former name of "*Chevau-Légers Lanciers de la Garde Impériale*". At the beginning of June 1815, at the beginning of the campaign, the war squadrons totalled 47 officers and 823 men.

Uniform

As was mentioned above, the Red Lancers were issued with a Polish-style uniform, after a lot of hesitation and trials, of which some example are shown in our plates. Apart from the background colour and that of the distinctives, there were some details which differentiated their uniforms from those of the 1ˢᵗ Regiment: the lapels of the kurtka were cut differently; in 1813, the bottom of the skirt had two small buttons, the trousers was less tight-fitting and did not having any lacing at the bottom of the legs. Note also that the Young Guard squadrons wore a kurtka with the inversed colours, with neither epaulette nor aglet and that the stripe on the shapska was only decorated with a simple N cut out of brass.

Equipment and armament

These were identical to those issued to the 1ˢᵗ Regiment.

Harnesses

These were identical to those of the Polish Chevau-Légers except for the colour of the buckles, the colour of the saddlecloth and its ornamentation. From 1811 onwards, the cloth shabrack was completed by a black sheepskin which was placed on top, thus forming a false removable mobile seat.

The Trumpeters

Except for the distinctive colours which were different, the silhouettes of the trumpeters of the 1ˢᵗ and 2ⁿᵈ Regiments of Chevau-Légers Lancers seem to be the same. In fact, the Red Lancers could be distinguished by several details: the colour of the plume was the other way around; they wore a gold cloth belt and narrow belt; their trousers and their shabrack had gold braid. As with the Poles, they had a service uniform which was sky blue.

The Officers

The Dutch officers had a lot of sumptuous uniforms, just like their Polish brothers-in-arms. But these uniforms got hem more than once into financial trouble. Indeed as mentioned above, they had to change uniforms three times! The plates show a variety of these brilliant and diverse items.

The EARLY UNIFORMS

Service dress for the Hussars of the Royal Dutch Guard, after Plate N°260 by Roger Forthoffer. It was wearing this uniform that the Dutch Hussars arrived in France in August 1810 to form the 2nd Regiment of Chevau-Légers Lancers of the Imperial Guard. The uniform conforms to the description given by Dumonceau, a Lieutenant in the corps in 1810.

New scarlet uniform adopted at the beginning of 1811, according to Lucien Rousselot's Plate N°68.

Dutch Hussar from the 3rd Regiment incorporated into the 2nd Regiment of Chevau-Légers Lancers, after P. Benigni. At the end of November 1810, the regiment not having yet got up to its theoretical strength, the ranks were filled with men taken from the 3rd Regiment of Dutch Hussars who kept their blue uniform until the new scarlet one was adopted at the beginning of 1811.

These two troopers have been taken from Commandant Bucquoy's series of cards devoted to the 2nd Regiment of Chevau-Légers Lancers of the Guard.

A uniform towards the end of 1810, after P. Benigni. It corresponds to the description given by Daru in his report to the Emperor on 9 August 1810 (scarlet coat and breeches) and to the prescriptions of the Decree of 13 September 1810: *"Article 8: Dress will remain the same except for the buttons which will be replaced by the buttons of our Guard, and the frogging will be removed."* According to the correspondence of certain officers in the corps, the "Hungarian-style" breeches and the blue waistcoats continued to be worn for some time afterwards.

41

FULL DRESS

The shapska was the same shape, size and decoration as that of the 1st Regiment but the colours were not: the crown was scarlet, the Russian braid, the braid of the turban and the cord with flounders were yellow and all the metal parts were made of brass, except for the silver background of the plate. One last detail: the cockade does not have a Maltese cross.

The uniform of the Chevau-Légers Lancers in the 2nd Regiment was identical to that worn by their Polish bothers-at-arms as far as the design was concerned. The top of the lapels of the Kurtka was slightly wider and ended in three points. In 1811, the bottom of the skirts did not have an extra button: these only appeared in 1813. The trousers were looser than those of the Poles and did not have lace tie-ups: the opening at the bottom was closed by means of a black leather strap under the arch of the foot fastening to a button. That's the cut dealt with! As far as the colours were concerned, the scarlet red already used by the Dutch Hussars was kept for the background and imperial blue was adopted for the distinctives because the sky blue was deemed to get dirty too easily.

Thanks to this rear view of the 1811 uniform, note the absence of a button in the folds at the bottom of the skirts. Note also the way the trouser legs were fastened: no lacing, but a button. Not also a detail which was specific to the 2nd Regiment of Chevau-Légers, shown by Lucien Rousselot on his Plate N°68: whilst the aglet is worn normally with one of the simple cords loose on the outside, the Red Lancers slipped the cord under the arm.

Chevau-Léger Lancer from the 2nd Regiment of the Imperial Guard in parade dress at the end of 1811.

FULL DRESS

Lancer wearing full dress according to the Weiland manuscript. It seems that here this is a transition uniform being tested.

Brigadier wearing full dress.

Brigadier wearing parade dress.

Trooper wearing full dress after the set of engravings by Martinet. It is reproduced in the collection of cards published by Commandant Bucquoy. On the original engraving, the front of the shabrack did not have a crowned "N" and the colours of the lance pennant were reversed.

Velite wearing full dress in 1811-1813. The Velite differed from his older brother-at-arms by his yellow trimmings mixed with dark blue and by his plume which was black with a white tip.

43

The YOUNG GUARD SQUADRONS

Brigadier from the squadrons of the Young Guard wearing town dress, according to Commandant Bucquoy.

Lancer from the squadrons of the Young Guard wearing full dress according to Plate N°68 by Lucien Rousselot.

Lancer from the squadrons of the Young Guard according to the aquarelles by Knötel.

The main difference between the uniform of the Chevau-Légers of the young Guard and that of their elders can be spotted immediately: the colours of their kurtka are inverted, imperial blue for the background and scarlet red for the distinctives. Moreover they wear neither epaulette nor aglet but rather two shoulder flaps made of blue cloth with red piping (Knötel) or two yellow fringeless epaulettes (Rousselot). Besides, they wore a less sumptuous shapska which according to Lucien Rousselot was simply decorated with an "N" cut out of brass on the front of the head band. As for Knötel, he drew it with the plaque with radiating lines. The strapping used by the Young Guard squadrons was not stitched. The cape-coat was similar to that of the Old Guard as far as the cut was concerned but it was made of ecru cloth. The last difference was that the shabrack was decorated with a single 2 1/8 inch stripe and had no outside piping. Knötel shows it with a simple stripe which seems to be narrower and blue outside piping.

CAMPAIGN DRESS

Chevau-Léger wearing guard dress (service dress), 1811-1813.

On the campaign uniform, the lapels on the kurtka were crossed. Riding breeches were worn; they were made of blue cloth with black veal-skin and a single scarlet stripe down each side. They were fastened down the side by eighteen brass buttons. They had two pockets of which the flaps facing upwards had red piping and five buttons each. The shapska was protected from the rain by a black oilskin.

Brigadier wearing summer marching dress. He is using stable canvas trousers instead of the riding breeches.

Stable dress.

Campaign dress towards 1812. The coat was worn over the shoulder from right to left so as not to get in the way of the lance or sabre during a charge.

Chevau-Léger of the Old Guard wearing a coat in 1812-1814.

CAMPAIGN DRESS

Trooper of the Old Guard in drill fatigues. He is wearing the jacket with the double row of buttons and riding breeches.

Trooper from the Young Guard wearing a coat. The squadrons of the Young Guard used a coat made of ecru cloth with a red collar. The forage cap and the trousers were identical to those worn by the veterans of the Old Guard.

Trooper from the Young Guard. With the marching uniform, the rear points of the shabrack were slipped under the holding belt and the sacks of oats were attached between the portmanteau and the cantle. The lance pennant is rolled up and protected by a black taffetas sheath.

At the beginning of the 1812 Campaign, the Chevau-Légers Lancers did not wear their kurtkas but their blue stable jackets with sleeves. This made the Emperor scold General de Colbert, their Commanding Officer. *"Do you honestly think that I have put the Lancers of my Guard into red clothes for them to keep them, so that they can go strutting around the Palais-Royal? Kindly get them to wear them."* Concerning the black sheepskin shabrack scalloped with red, opinion is divided as to whether or not it existed. This picture is taken from one of Commandant Bucquoy's cards drawn by Rousselot who repeated this interpretation on his plate N°68. Indeed, he thought that the famous black sheepskins were not big enough to cover the saddle holsters, the rolled up coat and the saddle and that they were only used as a removable seat placed over the shabrack.

ITEMS OF THE UNIFORM

Red Lancer's Kurtka. Round-edged epaulette with yellow wool fringes. Yellow woollen trefoil aglet, brass tags.

From 1813, two extra buttons were sewn onto the bottom of the skirts, partly hidden by the first fold.

Brigadier's kurtka. It has two yellow woollen stripes above the facing. This Brigadier has two seniority chevrons.

Shapska of the Young Guard squadrons.

Shapska of the Old Guard squadrons.

Forage cap with a blue head band and scarlet pendant with a yellow stripe for the troopers *(left)* and with a gold stripe for the NCOs *(right)*.

Shirt.

Brigadier-Fourrier's kurtka. The rank stripes were worn high up on the sleeves. *Maréchal-des-Logis'* aglet and epaulette.

Maréchal-des-Logis' kurtka. There is a single gold stripe above the facing. Aglet and epaulette are a mix of 1/3 gold and 2/3 red. The rounded edge of the epaulette was blue. Epaulette loops were gold.

Maréchal-des-Logis chef's kurtka. It has two gold stripes above the facing. Aglet and epaulette were a mix of 1/3 gold and 2/3 red. Rounded edge of epaulette was gold. Epaulette loops gold.

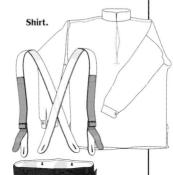

Half-bell Button.

The stable jacket with sleeves.

Fastening for the lower trouser legs (detail).

Short calf boots with iron spur screwed into the heel.

Marching trousers.

47

SADDLERY

Complete saddle and harness for the troopers and the NCOs of the squadrons of the Old Guard. The shabrack was decorated with two yellow stripes, one 2 1/4 inch wide and the other, 3/4 inch sewn inside the first. The outer edge of the shabrack had yellow piping. A black sheepskin lined and scalloped with yellow was placed over it making a false removable seat. Two crowned eagles embroidered with yellow wool decorated the tips. The shabracks used by the squadrons of the Young Guard had only one stripe; they had no piping and the false seat made of black sheepskin was not scalloped. During the First Restoration, the Imperial Eagles were replaced by the arms of France, which disappeared immediately afterwards to be replaced by the Eagle during the Hundred Days.

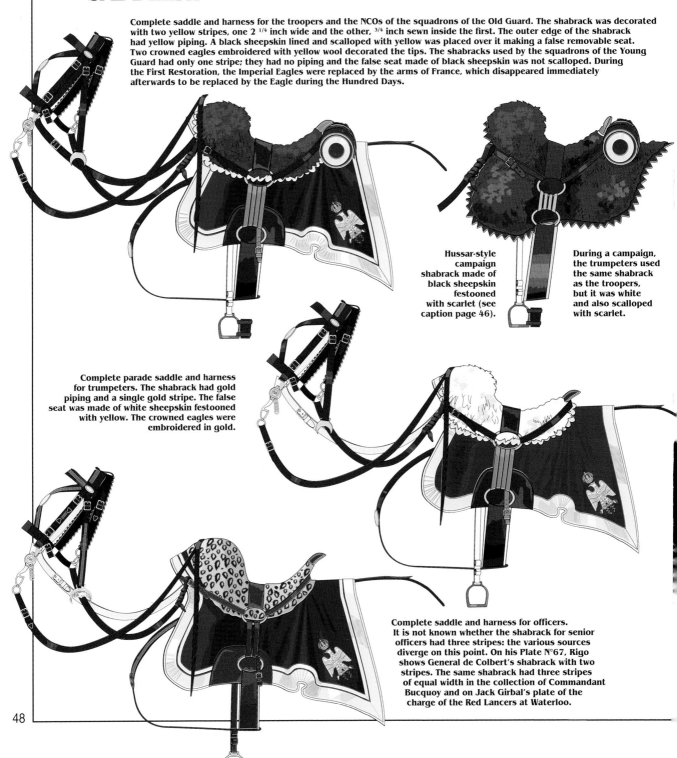

Hussar-style campaign shabrack made of black sheepskin festooned with scarlet (see caption page 46).

During a campaign, the trumpeters used the same shabrack as the troopers, but it was white and also scalloped with scarlet.

Complete parade saddle and harness for trumpeters. The shabrack had gold piping and a single gold stripe. The false seat was made of white sheepskin festooned with yellow. The crowned eagles were embroidered in gold.

Complete saddle and harness for officers. It is not known whether the shabrack for senior officers had three stripes: the various sources diverge on this point. On his Plate N°67, Rigo shows General de Colbert's shabrack with two stripes. The same shabrack had three stripes of equal width in the collection of Commandant Bucquoy and on Jack Girbal's plate of the charge of the Red Lancers at Waterloo.

The NON-COMMISSIONED OFFICERS

The NCOs in the squadrons of the Young Guard were recruited from the Old Guard or from the Line. In the first case, they kept their scarlet uniform and the distinctives of the Old Guard. For the NCOs from the Line, opinion is divided. P. Benigni thinks that they were given an Old Guard uniform; as for General Vanson, he thought that they wore the Old Guard distinctives but with a Young Guard uniform. One of the cards from Commandant Bucquoy's Collection, drawn by Lucien Rousselot after a sketch by General Vanson supports this idea.

Maréchal-des-Logis wearing summer town dress, 1813. He is wearing Polish-style nankeen or white cloth trousers.

Maréchal-des-Logis from the Young Guard squadrons wearing service dress after a drawing by General Vanson.

Kurtka worn by an *Adjudant-Sous-Officier*.
In 1814, the *Adjudant-Sous-Officier* replaced the *Lieutenant-Sous-Adjudant-Major* with the same duties. One of the cards in Commandant Bucquoy's Collection shows this adjutant's uniform but the gauntlet sleeves hide his stripes of rank. Most probably, there should be three stripes as this was the rule in the Light Cavalry. One has to be content with this uncertainty as there is no tangible proof in any of the sources, objects, or contemporary engravings to confirm this hypothesis.

Maréchal-des-Logis wearing full dress, 1811-1813.

Maréchal-des-Logis wearing campaign dress, 1811-1813, after one of Commandant Bucquoy's cards. Note that the shabrack does not have a false seat made of sheepskin, that it is decorated with a single stripe and that the front is decorated with a crowned "N".

49

TRUMPETERS IN FULL DRESS

Obverse and reverse sides of the pennant (called "étendard" in the documents of the period) of the 2nd the Chevau-Légers Lancer Regiment of the Guard. An example of this type is preserved in the Görlitz Museum. It comes from the Reichenbach battlefield which was the scene of a violent clash on 22 May 1813.

Trumpeter in full parade dress, 1812-1814.

The trumpeter's full dress uniform comprised a white kurtka with scarlet collar, lapels, facings and piping. The collar, the lapels and the facings were edged with a gold stripe ³/₄-inch wide. The lapel buttonholes are decorated with the same stripe. The epaulette and the aglet were identical to the NCOs'. The trousers were tailored in the same way as those of the troopers and were decorated with gold cord surrounded by two gold ³/₄-inch stripes on both sides. The shapska was garnished with white cloth, the Russian braid on the ridges was scarlet and a gold stripe covered the top of the turban. The plume was white with a scarlet tip. The NCO's cartridge case had copper sides and its flap was decorated with an eagle. The shoulder-strap was made of leather covered with red cloth onto which were sewn four gold stripes. On the front, it was decorated with a lion's head and an escutcheon stamped with an eagle, linked together by three little chains. The parade belt fastened on the side; it was made of red cloth decorated with four gold stripes which showed the background cloth. All the buckles were made of brass.

The trumpet cord and the tassels at the end were made up of 1/3 gold and 1/3 scarlet. The trumpeters were armed with the same sabre as the troopers but the sabre-knot had a mixed gold and scarlet tassel at the end.

Full parade dress kurtkas, trooper *(left)* and *Brigadier-Trompette (right)*, 1812-1814. The *Brigadier-Trompette* wore the stripes of the *Maréchal-des-Logis*. His collar was edged with a double gold stripe. The epaulette and the aglet were identical to those worn by all the trumpeters.

The TRUMPET-MAJOR

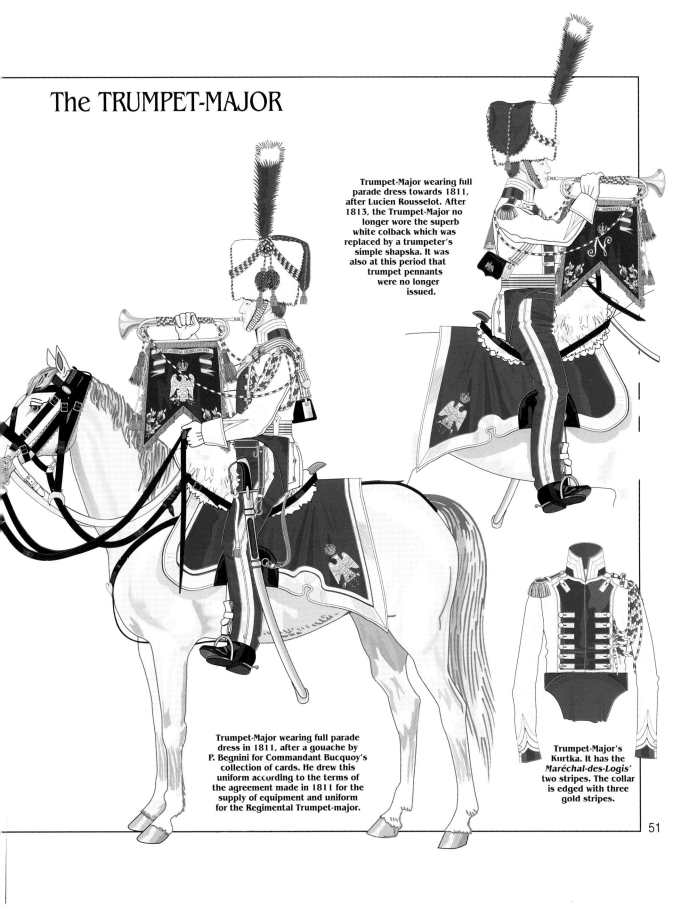

Trumpet-Major wearing full parade dress towards 1811, after Lucien Rousselot. After 1813, the Trumpet-Major no longer wore the superb white colback which was replaced by a trumpeter's simple shapska. It was also at this period that trumpet pennants were no longer issued.

Trumpet-Major wearing full parade dress in 1811, after a gouache by P. Begnini for Commandant Bucquoy's collection of cards. He drew this uniform according to the terms of the agreement made in 1811 for the supply of equipment and uniform for the Regimental Trumpet-major.

Trumpet-Major's Kurtka. It has the *Maréchal-des-Logis'* two stripes. The collar is edged with three gold stripes.

51

The TRUMPETER IN CAMPAIGN UNIFORM

Trumpeter wearing campaign uniform in 1813.

Trumpeter wearing campaign dress, 1812-1814.

Trumpeter wearing campaign dress, 1813 after one of Commandant Bucquoy's cards. As with the troopers the trumpeters used a sheepskin shabrack with the campaign uniform (see caption on page 46).

Trumpeter in service uniform after a drawing by P. Benigni. This second uniform was sky blue. The kurtka lapel button holes did not have any gold braid. The trousers were garnished with scarlet stripes and piping.

Trumpeter's kurtka (second uniform).

The TIMPANIST

For the Timpanist's uniform, we have based ourselves on Rigo's Plate N° 183 in *Le Plumet*; as sources, he himself used the drawings in Boersch's Collection. As a Strasbourg artist of the period, he probably came across the 2nd Regiment of Chevau-Légers Lancers at the time of their departure for the banks of the Niemen. The uniform was very similar to that of the Polish Chevau-Légers, except for the timpani aprons and the saddlecloth which seemed to be more soberly designed. There exists another version of this Timpanist's uniform in the Alsace Collection of card soldiers taken up by Commandant Bucquoy.

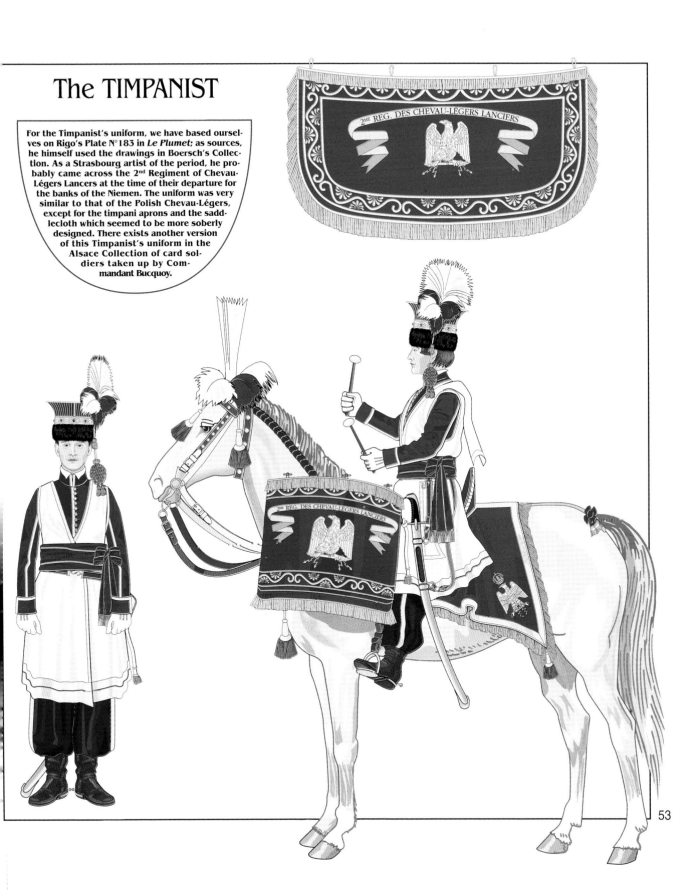

53

OFFICERS IN FULL DRESS

General de Colbert's Kurtka.
As he was of Major-General rank, on his ceremonial kurtka he wore the insignia of his rank: a double row of gold-embroidered oak leaves on the collar and the lapels. The flounders of the shapska cord, the top of the epaulettes and the sabre-knot tassel were decorated with three silver stars. The majors inthe regiment who held Major-General rank wore the same distinctions, but there was only one row of embroidery and only two stars.

Officer's kurtka and sash.
Only the epaulettes and their position distinguished the ranks from one another.

Officer wearing full parade dress.

General de Colbert, Colonel-Commandant of the regiment, wearing full dress, after Plate N° 67 by Rigo in *Le Plumet.*

Officer wearing full service dress.

OFFICERS IN SERVICE UNIFORM

Officer wearing marching uniform at the beginning of the Russian Campaign.

Officer wearing ballroom dress.

Officer wearing campaign uniform after a painting by General Lejeune showing the Battle of the Moskova (7 and 8 September 1812). He is wearing a coat-jacket in the form of a kurtka which buttons up straight on the chest. His buttoned riding breeches are garnished with a single gold stripe. This uniform can be called "full campaign dress" because the shapska has its plume and its cord and because he is wearing a belt with its plate and a full dress cartridge case. Besides, this and its shoulder-belt are not protected by the usual buttoned red morocco sheath. Note that there is no eagle in the shabrack corners and that the tips are decorated with gold-fringed tassels.

Officer wearing quarters dress according to a drawing by Lucien Rousselot made using a description of the period. He is wearing an overcoat and blue Polish-fashion gaiter-trousers, decorated with a simple red stripe.

55

EMBLEMS

VALEUR
ET DISCIPLINE
1ER ESCADRON

GARDE
IMPÉRIALE
L'EMPEREUR
DES FRANCAIS
AU 2ème RÉGIMENT
DES CHEV. LÉGERS
LANCIERS

1804-type standard received by the regiment during the 30 June 1811 parade.

Second-Lieutenant Henry Reckinger in 1815 during the Belgian campaign. He had been appointed Eagle-Bearer by the Imperial Decree of 22 May 1815.

Second-Lieutenant Jan Willem Verhaegen appointed Eagle-Bearer by the Imperial Decree of 30 October 1811, after Plate N°28 by Rigo in *Le Plumet*; note the baldric equipped with a hook for carrying the carbine which enabled the standard to be held in place.

GARDE
IMPÉRIALE
L'EMPEREUR
NAPOLÉON
AU 2ème RÉGIMENT
DE CHEVAU-LÉGERS
LANCIERS

1812-type standard received by the regiment in April 1813.

The 3rd CHEVAU-LEGERS LANCERS

The Imperial Decrees dated 5 and 10 July 1812 created the 3rd Chevau-Légers Lancer Regiment of the Guard at Grodno in Lithuania. It was organised in 5 two-company squadrons, but in the end only 4 squadrons were formed. As with the 1st Regiment, the recruitment of this cavalry was made among the better class young Poles and Lithuanians who could afford to equip themselves and furnish their own harnesses and equipment. The regiment was put on a war footing on 12 September 1812 and immediately left Warsaw for Russia. It headed for Minsk to join the Grande Armée on 5 October of the same year.

A fortnight later, in vaudeville-style circumstances where smugness rivalled with sheer incompetence, the regiment allowed itself to be surprised in the town of Slonim by the Russians.

The town was not even on the regiment's route. The wife of General Kopnaka, the regiment's commanding officer, and the wives of other officers lived in the town. The regiment deviated from its route and, forgetting to send out scouts and ignoring the "Grand Garde", the headquarters and several companies allowed themselves to be encircled by the Russians who were billeted only ten miles from the town. The General and most of the Lancers (i.e. the commanding officer, 13 officers and 235 troopers) were captured after a brief resistance. Thus the 3rd Regiment of Polish Chevau-Légers had a brief existence.

The horsemen who had escaped capture joined the 1st Regiment of Polish Chevau-Légers although they were allowed to keep their particularities.

After the disaster of the retreat from Russia and faced with the material impossibility of re-forming the 2nd Regiment of Polish Chevau-Légers, the survivors formed the 7th Squadron of the 1st Polish regiment of Chevau-Légers which had recently been reorganised.

The Uniform

The uniform was that worn by the Poles in the 1st Regiment: dark blue background and crimson distinctive. In order to distinguish the two regiments, the Lithuanians adopted yellow copper buttons.

Since traditionally, yellow copper was not to be mixed with white striping – and vice-versa – all the

Chevau-léger Lancer from the 3rd Regiment wearin full dress.

trimmings were yellow for the troopers and gold for the officers.

However, a kurtka from the 3rd Regiment, preserved in the Moscow History Museum would tend to prove the opposite; unless of course this veteran of the 3rd Regiment had kept his yellow buttons on his kurtka after joining the 1st Regiment. This of course remains hypothetical.

57

The 3rd CHEVAU-LEGERS LANCERS

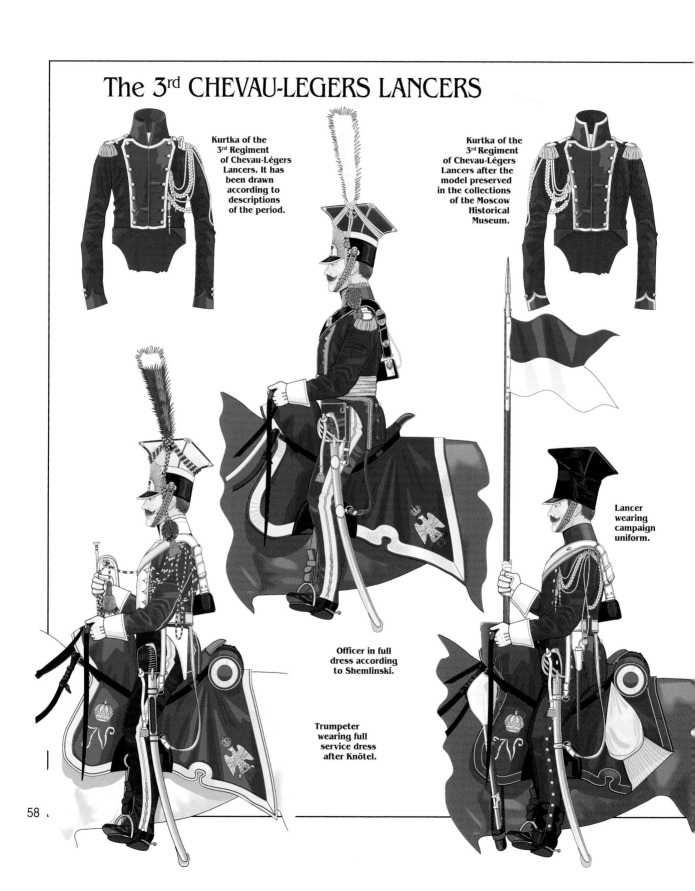

Kurtka of the 3rd Regiment of Chevau-Légers Lancers. It has been drawn according to descriptions of the period.

Kurtka of the 3rd Regiment of Chevau-Légers Lancers after the model preserved in the collections of the Moscow Historical Museum.

Lancer wearing campaign uniform.

Officer in full dress according to Shemlinski.

Trumpeter wearing full service dress after Knötel.

The BERG LANCERS

The Duchy of Cleves was ceded to France by Prussia according to the clauses in the Treaty of Schonbrunn on 15 December 1805. On 8 March 1806, Napoleon announced that the two Duchies of Cleves and Berg would be merged together. The title of Duke was granted to Joachim Murat, who entered Düsseldorf on 24 March with a French administration in his luggage whose orders were to govern the Duchy along French lines. This new state was in fact to serve as a buffer between France and Prussia. On 12 July 1806, Murat was officially crowned Grand-Duke of Berg and he incorporated it into the Rhine Confederation, thus breaking all links with the Holy Roman Empire. In fact, all the Grand-Duchy's business was dealt with from Paris, by Maret under the Emperor's watchful eye. In exchange, the Grand-Duke promised to supply a contingent of 5 000 men for all the continental wars in which the French Empire would be engaged.

The Grand-Duke was allowed to create a regiment of Chevau-Légers for his personal guard. These horsemen, all volunteers, were recruited from among the more prosperous people in the Duchy.

On 5 April 1808, only one squadron and one company were ready. The "new regiment" was immediately sent to Spain to join the handsome Joachim – who, need one be reminded, was Napoleon's brother-in-law – who was impatient to be crowned King of Spain. Unfortunately for him, the Emperor of the French's family sensitivity did not extend so far, and it was Joseph, the future "Pepe Botello", who ended up on the throne left vacant by the Bourbons.

Murat immediately left Spain for Naples, which was just as sunny a consolation prize, and where at last there was a throne, waiting just for him.

However, the Chevau-Légers stayed in Madrid where Napoleon incorporated them into his Guard in November 1808. The unit was very quickly disbanded and the horsemen incorporated into the *Chasseurs à cheval* of the Guard. A second unit was set up by Count Beugnot, the Administrator of the Grand-Duchy in Murat's absence. It took the name of the Berg *Chasseurs à cheval*. This light cavalry was armed with lances and put into the expert hands of instructors seconded from the Polish Lancers of the Guard. The regiment very logically became the Berg Lancers and just as logically attached to the Guard. They set off immediately for Spain.

Between the Yanguas affair on 6 September 1809 – their first engagement – and the Battle of Villafranca, on 26 December 1810, they lost a third of their strength. They continued their struggle against the guerrillas in the Peninsula, chasing Spanish partisans and cutting up English squares until 1813. A second regiment of Berg Chevau-Légers Lancers was formed in Germany in preparation for the Russian Campaign. Only two companies of horsemen survived the disastrous retreat.

The survivors of the retreat from Russia and those from Spain formed a squadron under the command of General de Colbert. They made up a brigade with the Lancers of the Guard during the German Campaign. The Battle of Leipzig (16 October 1813), fought alongside the Polish Lancers of the Guard, tolled the knell of the Berg lancers.

The Uniform

There were two quite distinct uniforms. The white uniform of the first period (1807-1808) was distinguished by the amarante pink which could have been a dark pink. Although this "Polish-style" uniform was well and truly drawn by Baron Lejeune, nobody can today confirm whether it was ever really worn. The position of the aglet for example, first on the right then on the left varies from one source to another; it was more logical to place it on the right since these first generation Chevau-Légers were not equipped with a lance.

The full dress uniform was completed by an entirely grey campaign uniform with a shapska cover made of black waxed cloth.

The Berg Lancers' second uniform also had a Polish cut. The coat's background colour was *chasseur* green with an amarante pink distinctive.

The horsemen in the 1st Company of the 1st Squadron (the Elite Company) in full dress wore a pair of red epaulettes and a colback with a red plume until 1813.

The shapska and the shako were worn in the regimental companies and now it seems that they were issued according to certain rules. Some sources indicate that the shako was worn in Spain.

The breeches were "Hungarian-style", worn with the little boots of the Polish Chevau-Légers. When campaigning, riding trousers were worn.

Equipment was the same as for the Light Cavalry.

They used a "Hungarian-style" saddle, covered for the centre companies with an amarante pink shabrack edged with a black and white stripe. This lay-out can be seen in Knötel's set of drawings.

59

The BERG CHEVAU-LEGERS

Kurtka belonging to the bodyguard of the Grand-Duke of Berg.

Kurtka belonging to Chevau-Léger of the Grand-Duke of Berg.

Chevau-Léger of the Grand-Duke of Berg wearing full dress.

NCO from the bodyguard wearing full dress according to Knötel.

The letter "J" (for Joachim) which decorated the portmanteau and the shabrack was Murat's monogramme.

Officer from the bodyguard in full dress. It seems that the main difference between the uniform of the Chevau-Légers and that of the bodyguards lay in the frogging which decorated the latter's lapels.

The BERG CHEVAU-LEGERS TRUMPETERS

Trumpeters from the Berg Chevau-Légers wearing full dress. As was the custom in the cavalry, the uniform colours were reversed compared with those of the troopers. The mounted trumpeter has been given a white metal trumpet matching the trimmings (which were a mix of silver and white) better. But this is only a hypothesis. The apron decorated with an eagle on the dismounted trumpeter's instrument was inspired by the one drawn by Jack Girbal for a plate in Dr Hourtoulle's Collection. No picture of the reverse side of this apron in known to exist.

The BERG CHEVAU-LEGERS

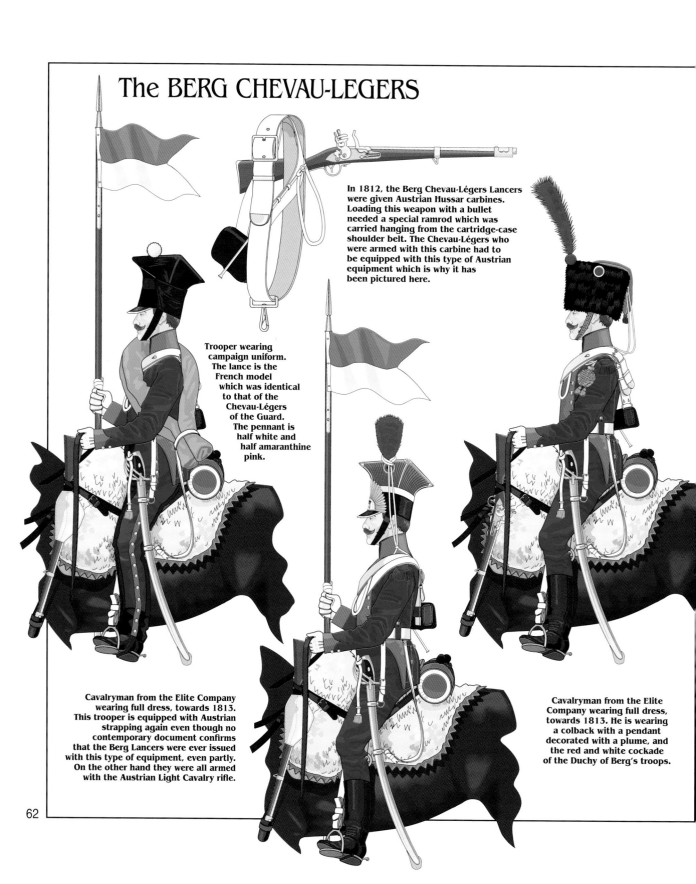

In 1812, the Berg Chevau-Légers Lancers were given Austrian Hussar carbines. Loading this weapon with a bullet needed a special ramrod which was carried hanging from the cartridge-case shoulder belt. The Chevau-Légers who were armed with this carbine had to be equipped with this type of Austrian equipment which is why it has been pictured here.

Trooper wearing campaign uniform. The lance is the French model which was identical to that of the Chevau-Légers of the Guard. The pennant is half white and half amaranthine pink.

Cavalryman from the Elite Company wearing full dress, towards 1813. This trooper is equipped with Austrian strapping again even though no contemporary document confirms that the Berg Lancers were ever issued with this type of equipment, even partly. On the other hand they were all armed with the Austrian Light Cavalry rifle.

Cavalryman from the Elite Company wearing full dress, towards 1813. He is wearing a colback with a pendant decorated with a plume, and the red and white cockade of the Duchy of Berg's troops.

The BERG CHEVAU-LEGERS

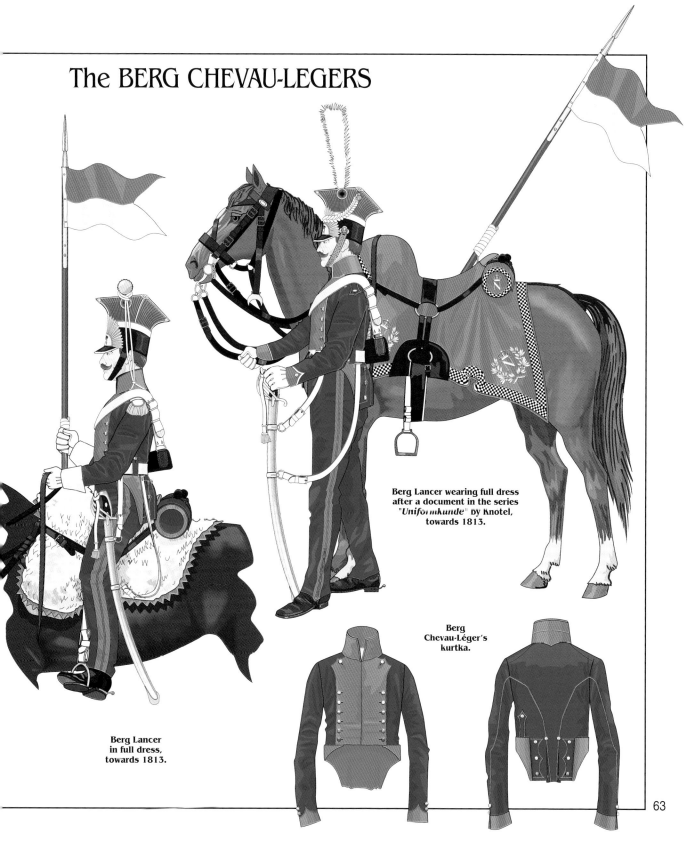

Berg Lancer wearing full dress
after a document in the series
"Uniformkunde" by Knotel,
towards 1813.

Berg
Chevau-Léger's
kurtka.

Berg Lancer
in full dress,
towards 1813.

The BERG CHEVAU-LEGERS

The stripe garnishing the Imperial livery for the trumpeters was woven in two ways: horizontal and vertical. This was so that it could be "read" no matter where it was placed on the uniform.

Uniform worn in Spain. This was the uniform for the *Chasseurs de Berg:* created on 29 August 1809 and changed into Lancers on 17 December of the same year. They left for Spain in 1810 and kept their *Chasseurs à Cheval* uniform.

Two trumpeters from the Berg Chevau-Légers Lancers wearing Imperial livery according to the 1812 regulations. The one above is taken from the series of aquarelles by R. Knötel. The one on the right is taken from one of the plates drawn by Jack Girbal for Dr Hourtoulle's set of uniforms. They are wearing the same uniform as the troopers, but it is decorated with the Imperial livery braid stripe, with a pair of white epaulettes. The amaranthine shapska of Knötel's trumpeter probably indicates the first regiment and Girbal's green shapska, the second. The trumpeter on the right is wearing a pair of "mixed grey" riding breeches: this colour was supposed to be for the campaign uniform.

The GENDARMERIE D'ÉLITE

The Decree of 29 July 1804 (10 Thermidor Year XII) dealt with the reorganisation and transformation of the Consular Guard which became the Imperial Guard. The composition of this new unit did not change. The Gendarmes' principal task was to maintain law and order in all the places where the Government, and of course the Emperor, were located. As a result, they took part in all the Empire's campaigns anywhere the General Headquarters was located.

Their duties included:

A mounted Guard for the Tuileries Palace and the Malmaison, as well as a courier service, and the security of the Emperor's carriage, a security post on the terrace of the Tuileries Palace, on the garden side; and two security posts at the Temple Prison.

The other duties consisted of ensuring the Emperor's security and that of his entourage while travelling, escort duties and the safety of the high dignitaries and heads of foreign states visiting Imperial territory.

While campaigning, the Gendarmes were incorporated into the Cavalry of the Guard. They guarded the prisoners and the trophies. All the duties and the services of the Provost at General Headquarters were taken on by the Legion. During the Russian Campaign, they were given the task of gathering in any laggards back into the army.

Composition

The Gendarmerie d'Elite Legion comprised two mounted two-company squadrons and a half battalion of two companies on foot, a total strength of 633 men with their headquarters. The Gendarmes d'Elite were all NCOs who came from the troop corps. The battalion on foot was disbanded on 15 April 1806.

A "second series" of Gendarmes, the "Gendarmes-bis" was created in 1813. They were immediately assigned to the Young Guard. The Decree of 1 March 1813 increased their strength to 1 174 men. 160 "Gendarmes-cadets" entered the Guard by the Decree of 16 January 1814.

During the First Restoration, the Gendarmerie d'Elite Corps was disbanded on 23 April 1814. Louis XVIII created a Company of the "Gendarmes des Chasses du Roi" which included part of the Gendarmes d'Elite of the former Imperial Guard. When Napoleon returned, the Gendarmerie d'Elite was re-incorporated into the Guard. When the Guard was reorganised on 8 April 1815, the Gendarmes were 100-strong; their strength increased to 250, made up mainly of former Gendarmes of the Guard, of Gendarmes from the Legions inside France and the "Gendarmes of the Chasses du Roi". A detachment of the Gendarmerie took part in the Battle of Ligny and then Waterloo. On 26 September 1815, the Gendarmerie d'Elite was dismissed at Châtellerault.

The uniform

The coat was made of imperial blue cloth tailored in the same style as the Grenadiers à cheval with a blue collar and scarlet lapels, facings and turnbacks. The opening of the pockets was cut at a slant and the turnbacks decorated with blue grenades. The buttons

---

The GENDARMES D'ÉLITE

The Headquarters comprised:
— 1 Colonel
— 1 Majors
— 2 Squadron Commanders (one on foot)
— 1 Quartermaster
— 1 Adjudant-Major
— 2 Under Adjudant-Majors (one on foot)
— 2 Health Officers
— 2 Standard-bearers
— 1 Flag-Bearer
— 1 Veterinary Officer
— 12 Musicians
— 1 Master-Tailor and Gaiter-maker
— 1 Master-Saddler
— 1 Master-Breech-maker
— 1 Master-Boot-maker
— 1 Master-Armourer and Spur-maker

Each of the **mounted squadrons** comprised:
— 2 First-Lieutenants
— 1 Maréchal-des-logis Chef
— 1 Maréchal-des-Logis
— 1 Fourrier
— 6 Brigadiers
— 72 Gendarmes
— 2 Trumpeters
— 1 Blacksmith

Each of the **companies on foot** comprised:
— 1 Captain
— 2 Lieutenants
— 1 Maréchal-des-Logis Chef
— 5 Maréchaux-des-Logis
— 1 Fourrier
— 10 Brigadiers
— 100 Gendarmes
— 2 Drummers

were made of white metal stamped with the eagle of the Guard. The trefoil shoulder flaps (worn on the right) and the aglet (worn on the left) were braided with white thread.

The service dress overcoat was made of blue cloth with five buttons with straight facings. The piping on the collars, the fronts, the lining and turnbacks were scarlet. The jacket was made of chamois cloth; the full dress breeches were made of buckskin; a second pair of breeches was made of sheepskin and used for everyday dress. Both of them were yellow ochre. While marching or campaigning over-breeches fastening on the side made of ecru cloth were worn over the skin breeches. Breeches made of blue cloth were used for quarters dress and for town dress. The coat with a cape and sleeves was imperial blue and had three buttonholes with white braid. Stable dress comprised a jacket with two rows of cloth buttons and fatigue trousers.

From 1801 to 1804 the Gendarmes wore a black felt hat trimmed with white braid; the braid of the cockade and the fringed "marrons" were also silver. In full dress, the hat had a scarlet plume. They were also issued with a second hat for service dress. A blue forage cap with red frogs and a tassel made of white thread; the headband was decorated with two white stripes and a grenade made of white cloth.

In 1806 a black bearskin hat with a visor and strap replaced the hat; the outer reinforcement of the visor and the scales on the chinstrap were made of white metal. The scarlet background was decorated with a white grenade. A red (or white depending on the period) plume, a tricolour pompon-cockade and a simple cord made of white thread, with two flounders and three tassels completed the hat. Between 1804 and 1808-1809, the "Gendarmes à Cheval" used semi-stiff boots with knee pieces for parade dress; then they were given stiff boots with smooth calves. For ordinary service dress they were given soft boots. The spurs were made of blackened iron. For quarters or exercise dress they wore a pair of gaiters.

Equipment

The belt, the cartridge-case shoulder-belt and the musket shoulder-belt were made of yellowed hide and edged with a white thread braid; all the rest of the strappings were yellow. The belt-plate decorated with

an embossed grenade was made of brass. The gauntlets were yellow ochre. The flap of the cartridge case was made of black leather but its exact shape is not known but it was decorated with a yellow brass grenade; it was replaced in 1806 by a crowned eagle.

Weapons

The Gendarmes à Cheval were issued with a sabre and a pair of pistols, the "Gendarmes à Pied" with an Infantry sabre; all of them were armed with a musketoon and a bayonet.

The sabre with a straight-edged blade was that of the Cavalry of the Line, first the An IX model then the An XI model with an iron scabbard. In about 1806-1807 the Gendarmerie d'Elite received the Guard "Grenadiers à Cheval" sabre.

The pistols were first the An IX model then the An XII model. Various models of musketoons were used: at the beginning of the Empire, the Gendarmes still used the cavalry 1763-66 model or the "Maréchaussée" 1770-model musketoon; they were then issued with the An IX then the An XIII models.

Harnesses

The "French-style" of harness was used; the saddle and the holsters were made of tawny leather; all the leather was black and the buckles were made of brass. The studs of the bridle bit were stamped with a grenade. The saddlecloth and the flaps were made of dark blue cloth. The tips were decorated with a grenade made of white thread; this was replaced by a crown in 1807. In full dress, the white fillet replaced the black fillet. The portmanteau was rectangular not round and made of blue cloth; its ends had white braid. Up to 1807, a similarly-shaped bag was placed on top of the portmanteau; it was held in place by a long flap on the portmanteau which covered and held everything in place. The coat was folded like a wallet with the lining showing and was placed on top of the portmanteau and bag. The ends of the portmanteaux issued after 1807 had double white braid.

We will show the trumpeters, the drummers, the musicians and the officers of the Gendarmerie d'Elite in Volume 4 of the present collection. This will continue the study of the Cavalry of the Guard.

The COMPANIES ON FOOT, 1804-1806

Campaign uniform 1804-1806.
The colour of the pompon indicated the rank of the company. Unfortunately the detail of how the colours were assigned is not known.

Town dress in 1804-1806.

Uniform including the greatcoat, 1804-1806.

Full summer uniform, 1804-1806.

Maréchal-des-Logis wearing a greatcoat, 1804-1806.
The braid on the buttonholes of the greatcoat was a mix of blue and silver. The exact design is not known.

The Gendarmes in the Companies on foot (Compagnies à pied) were issued with the same uniform as the Gendarmes à Cheval, except for the following details: two red goat's hair epaulettes replaced the trefoil and the aglet; they had two pairs of gaiters, one black and the other white; in service dress, they used a pair of blue canvas trousers worn over the gaiters.

The "GENDARME À PIED", 1804-06

"French-style" coat and epaulettes for the "Gendarmes à Pied".

In 1804, the grenades on the turnbacks were blue. They were white after 1806.

Overcoat. It was fastened by means of 5 buttons and cut higher up on the chest than those of the other corps.

Full winter "à pied" uniform with the black gaiters. In summer they wore white gaiters. The "Gendarme à Pied" was armed with a musketoon and bayonet, and with an Infantry of the Line sabre.

Epaulette worn by all three ranks.

Breeches and tunic. The latter has sleeves and was made from chamois cloth like the breeches.

1   2   3

Rank stripes:
1. Brigadier.
2. Maréchal-des-Logis.
3. Maréchal-des-Logis Chef.

The button with the eagle belongs to the Guard.

The "GENDARME À PIED", 1804-1806

Drummer wearing summer full-dress, 1808. Two versions of the shoulder trefoils used in the Consular Guard are shown.

Drummer in 1804. Except for the buttons stamped with an eagle, the uniform was the same as that worn in the Gendarmerie.

Subaltern. He was the only officer in the "Gendarmes à Pied" Regiment to wear an aglet. This man here was armed with either a sword or a Grenadier's sabre.

Gendarme à Pied's full equipment. Sabre-holder baldric, cartridge case shoulder belt and cartridge case. At the beginning of the Empire, the flap on the case was decorated with a grenade which was then replaced by an eagle. The backpack was the Infantry of the Guard model. All the leather strapping was yellow.

"GENDARMERIE A CHEVAL", FULL DRESS UNIFORMS

Before 1808, the horses were chestnut; subsequently, they were black or brown bays like those of the Grenadiers à Cheval. The trumpeters' mounts were grey.

Full dress in 1804. The Gendarme was armed with the cavalry of the Line An IX-model sabre and, probably, with the 1763-66-model musketoon with bayonet.

Full dress in 1806. This Gendarme is carrying the Cavalry of the Line An XI-model sabre and An IX-model musketoon with bayonet.

Full dress in 1808. The coat's turnbacks were sewn so that the triangle was no longer visible as it had been up until then. The grenade on the turnback was white like the plume. The boots had smooth, firm calves.

This Gendarme is carrying the Grenadier à Cheval of the Guard sabre. There is a crown made of embroidered white thread in the rear corners of the saddlecloth. The portmanteau has been simplified: it has lost its pouch and has been edged with two white thread braid stripes.

CAMPAIGN UNIFORMS

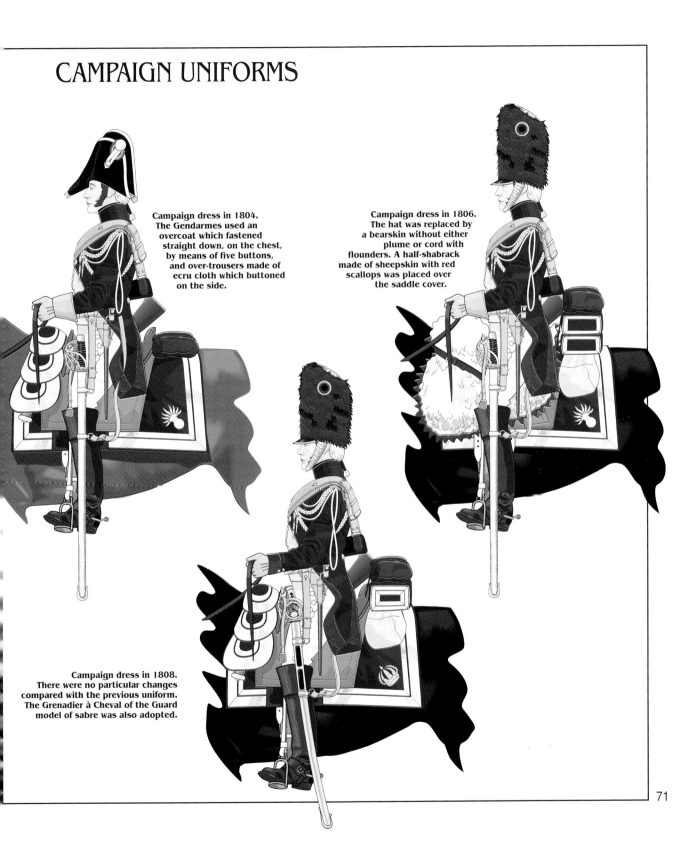

Campaign dress in 1804.
The Gendarmes used an
overcoat which fastened
straight down, on the chest,
by means of five buttons,
and over-trousers made of
ecru cloth which buttoned
on the side.

Campaign dress in 1806.
The hat was replaced by
a bearskin without either
plume or cord with
flounders. A half-shabrack
made of sheepskin with red
scallops was placed over
the saddle cover.

Campaign dress in 1808.
There were no particular changes
compared with the previous uniform.
The Grenadier à Cheval of the Guard
model of sabre was also adopted.

CAMPAIGN UNIFORMS

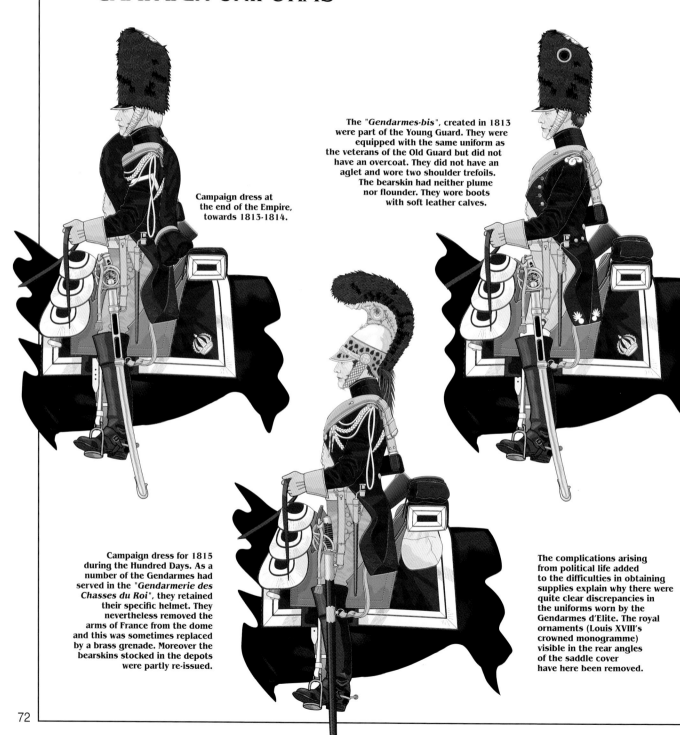

Campaign dress at the end of the Empire, towards 1813-1814.

The "*Gendarmes-bis*", created in 1813 were part of the Young Guard. They were equipped with the same uniform as the veterans of the Old Guard but did not have an overcoat. They did not have an aglet and wore two shoulder trefoils. The bearskin had neither plume nor flounder. They wore boots with soft leather calves.

Campaign dress for 1815 during the Hundred Days. As a number of the Gendarmes had served in the "*Gendarmerie des Chasses du Roi*", they retained their specific helmet. They nevertheless removed the arms of France from the dome and this was sometimes replaced by a brass grenade. Moreover the bearskins stocked in the depots were partly re-issued.

The complications arising from political life added to the difficulties in obtaining supplies explain why there were quite clear discrepancies in the uniforms worn by the Gendarmes d'Elite. The royal ornaments (Louis XVIII's crowned monogramme) visible in the rear angles of the saddle cover have here been removed.

UNIFORM FOR THE "GENDARMES A PIED"

Full service dress "à pied",
1807-1814.

Gendarme wearing
an overcoat towards
1808 after Plate N°95
by Lucien Rousselot.
The artist's principle
source was a
contemporary
document by
the famous
Hendschel.

Summer town dress,
1807-1814.

Winter town dress,
1807-1814.

UNIFORM FOR THE *"GENDARMES A PIED"*

Gendarme
wearing
a greatcoat,
1804.

"Garde à pied"
Uniform,
1807-1814.

Gendarme
wearing
a greatcoat,
1808-1814.

Gendarme-Cadet in 1814.
When they entered the Guard
they kept their coat and
overcoat. The rest of their
clothing was identical
to that worn by the
"Gendarmes-bis".

Gendarme « bis »
in 1813.

74

STABLE AND TRAINING UNIFORMS

Mounted training uniform
worn at the Boulogne camp
in 1804, after a draxing
by P. Benigni. The big blue
cover was not used:
it was replaced by
a blanket which
was slipped under
the saddle.

Two types of stable
dress worn by the
Gendarmes d'Elite.
Top: in winter.
Right: in summer.

Summer "*à pied*"
training uniform.

CLOTHING

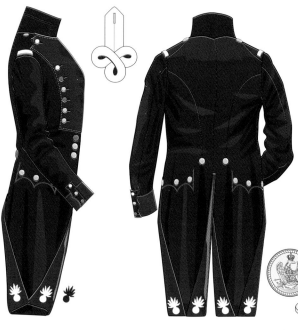

Overcoat. The stripes of rank worn on the overcoat were not edged with red.

Button with the eagle of the Guard.

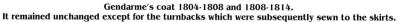

Gendarme's coat 1804-1808 and 1808-1814.
It remained unchanged except for the turnbacks which were subsequently sewn to the skirts.

Brigadier.

Maréchal-des-logis.

Maréchal-des-logis chef.

The sleeveless waistcoat was made of yellow cloth.

Forage cap worn by the Gendarmes *(left)* and the NCOs *(right)* in the Corps.

Riding breeches made of ochre deerskin.

The leg cuff was made of reinforced cloth in order to prevent the breeches from being worn by the rubbing of the boots.

ARMAMENT and EQUIPMENT

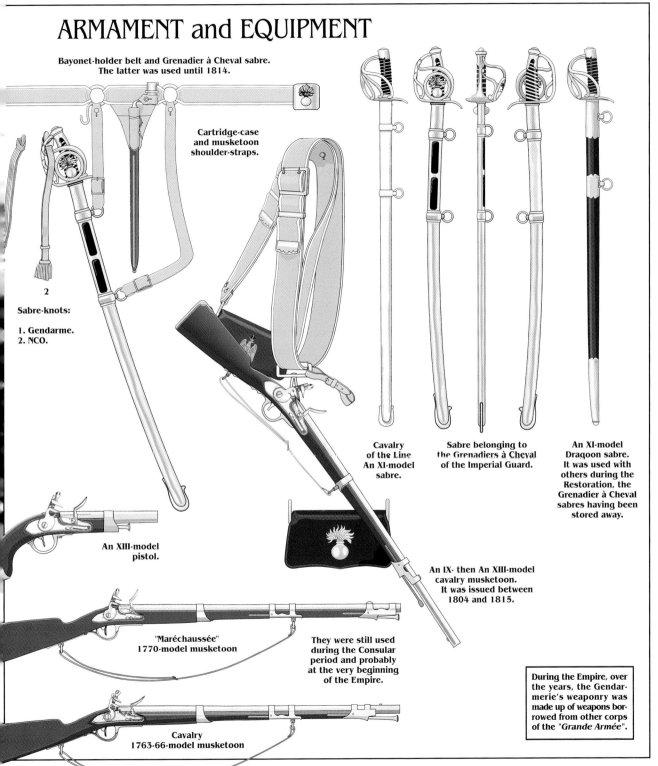

Bayonet-holder belt and Grenadier à Cheval sabre. The latter was used until 1814.

Cartridge-case and musketoon shoulder-straps.

2

Sabre-knots:

1. Gendarme.
2. NCO.

An XIII-model pistol.

Cavalry of the Line An XI-model sabre.

Sabre belonging to the Grenadiers à Cheval of the Imperial Guard.

An XI-model Dragoon sabre. It was used with others during the Restoration, the Grenadier à Cheval sabres having been stored away.

An IX- then An XIII-model cavalry musketoon. It was issued between 1804 and 1815.

"Maréchaussée" 1770-model musketoon

They were still used during the Consular period and probably at the very beginning of the Empire.

Cavalry 1763-66-model musketoon

During the Empire, over the years, the Gendarmerie's weaponry was made up of weapons borrowed from other corps of the *Grande Armée*.

77

SADDLERY

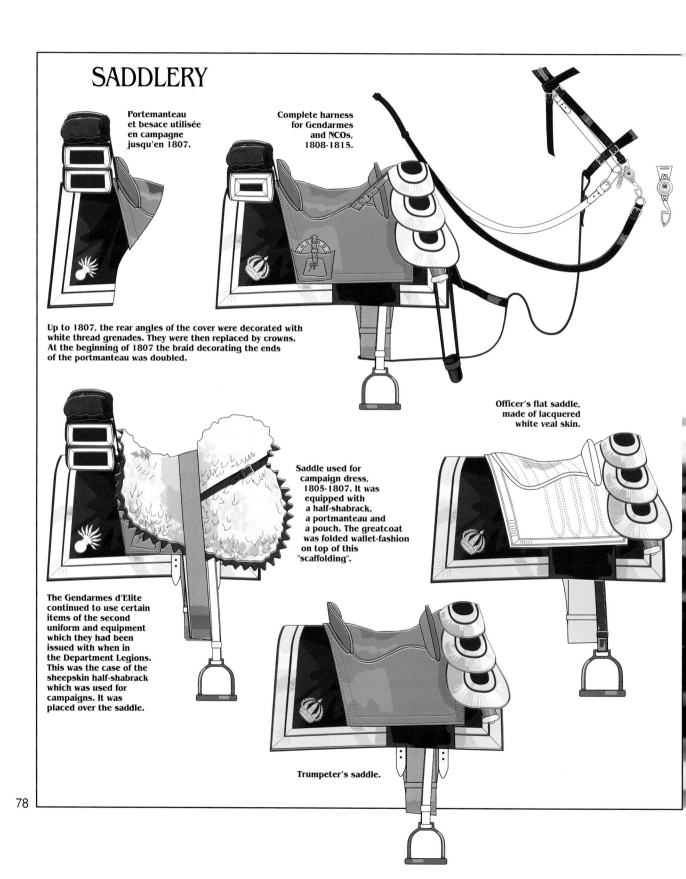

Portemanteau et besace utilisée en campagne jusqu'en 1807.

Complete harness for Gendarmes and NCOs, 1808-1815.

Up to 1807, the rear angles of the cover were decorated with white thread grenades. They were then replaced by crowns. At the beginning of 1807 the braid decorating the ends of the portmanteau was doubled.

Saddle used for campaign dress, 1805-1807. It was equipped with a half-shabrack, a portmanteau and a pouch. The greatcoat was folded wallet-fashion on top of this "scaffolding".

Officer's flat saddle, made of lacquered white veal skin.

The Gendarmes d'Elite continued to use certain items of the second uniform and equipment which had been issued with when in the Department Legions. This was the case of the sheepskin half-shabrack which was used for campaigns. It was placed over the saddle.

Trumpeter's saddle.

The NON-COMMISSIONED OFFICERS

From the rank of Briga-
dier upwards, the Gen-
darme could be distin-
guished by the silver and
blue aglet, the silver shoulder trefoil and the mixed
silver and blue sabre-knot.

Maréchal-des-Logis
wearing an overcoat,
1804.

Brigadier wearing
"Garde à pied"
Uniform,
1804.

Maréchal-des-Logis
wearing full dress,
1808-1814.

Brigadier
wearing
Town dress,
1807-1814.

Maréchal-des-Logis
wearing full dress,
1806-1808

79

The NON-COMMISSIONED OFFICERS

Brigadier wearing campaign dress towards the end of the Empire.

Maréchal-des-Logis Chef from the **"Compagnies à Pied"**, wearing town dress and overcoat, 1805.

Maréchal-des-Logis in *"à pied"* service dress, 1806-1814.

NCO wearing a frock coat, 1806-1815. This item of clothing was issued to all NCOs.

Brigadier wearing *"à pied"* service dress, 1815.

The TRUMPETER

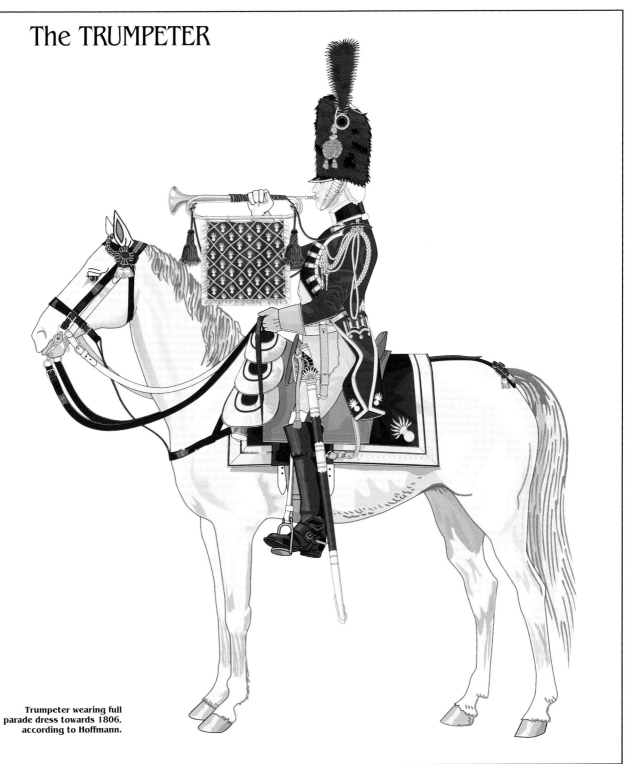

Trumpeter wearing full parade dress towards 1806, according to Hoffmann.

BIBLIOGRAPHY

Planches « Uniformes de l'Armée française » par Lucien Rousselot
— Chevau-légers polonais. Planches n° 47, n° 65 et n° 75.
— 2e Chevau-légers. Planches n° 68, et n° 88.
— La Gendarmerie d'élite. Planche n° 95.

Planches « Le Plumet » par Rigo
— Timbalier des mameluks. Planche n° 101.
— Guidon des mameluks. Planche n° 32.
— Porte-étendard du 2e Chevau-légers. Planche n° 28.
— Colonel du 2e Chevau-égers. Planche n° 67.
— Le timbalier du 2e Chevau-légers. Planche n° 183.
— Chevau-légers polonais. Planches n° 36 et n° 25.

Livres
— Soldats et uniformes du Premier Empire,
Dr F.-G. Hourtoulle, J. Girbal ; P. Courcelle. *Histoire & Collections.*
— La Garde Impériale,
L. Fallou. *Editions J. Olmes* (réédition).
— Armes à feu réglementaires françaises 1717-1836,
J. Boudriot.
— Equipement militaire. 1600 1870.Tome IV
M. Pétard. *Chez l'auteur*
— Drapeaux et étendards du Premier Empire,
P. Charrié. *Editions Copernic.*
— Garde Impériale, Mameluks,
Collection Raoul et Jean Brunon, Marseille.
— Les Polonais de Napoléon,
J. Tranié et Carmigniani, *Editions Copernic.*

— Les lanciers rouges, Ronald Pawly, *De Krijger.*
— Guide à l'usage des costumiers,
H. Malibran.
— La Garde impériale. Les troupes à cheval,
Commandant Bucquoy. *Editions Grancher.*
— Napoléon et ses soldats,
Collection historique du Musée de l'Armée. *Editions Préal.*
— Manuscrit du camp de Dresde,
Sauerweid. *Editions Pierre Brétegnier.*
— Dictionnaire du consulat et de l'Empire,
J. Tulard. *Editions Fayard.*
— Les uniformes et armes des soldats du Premier Empire,
L. & F. Funcken. *Editions Castermann.*
— Napoléon's Elite cavalry,
L. Rousselot & E. Ryan. *Editions Greenhill Books.*
— Napoleon's army,
A. Martinet & G, Dempsey. *Editions Greenhill Books.*
— Napoleonic uniforms,
J. Elting & R. Knötel. *Editions MacMillan.*

Revues
— Le gendarme d'élite
M. Pétard in *Uniformes* n° 90.
— Le lancier polonais
M. Pétard in *Uniformes* n° 77.
— La compagnie de mameluks
J. Chambenoit in *bulletin du CFFH 2004/1.*

ACKNOWLEDGEMENTS

We would like to thank *Rigo, Michel Pétard, Dr François-Guy Hourtoulle, M. Lapray* and *Jean-Louis Viau* for their precious help as much morale-wise as editorially.
We would like to pay them the tribute which they deserve.

Design, creation, lay-out and realisation by ANDRE JOUINEAU and JEAN-MARIE MONGIN.
Re-reading and updating DENIS GANDILHON and JEAN-LOUIS VIAU. © *Histoire & Collections* 2005
Computer Drawings by André JOUINEAU

SA au capital de 182 938,82 €

5, avenue de la République
F-75541 Paris Cédex 11
Téléphone : 01 40 21 18 20
Fax :   01 47 00 51 11

This book has been designed, typed
laid-out and processed
by *Histoire & Collections*
fully on integrated computer equipment

Printed by ZURE
Spain, European Union